Effective resolution of collective labour disputes

Europa Law Publishing, Groningen 2006

Effective resolution of collective labour disputes

Edited by

A.F.M. Brenninkmeijer L.C.J. Sprengers

A.J. de Roo R.W. Jagtenberg

Europa Law Publishing is a publishing company specializing in European Union law, international trade law, public international law, environmental law and comparative national law.
For further information please contact Europa Law Publishing via email: info@europalawpublishing.com or visit our website at: www.europalawpublishing.com.

Typeset in Scala and Scala Sans, Graphic design by G2K Designers, Groningen/Amsterdam

NUR 825
ISBN-10: 90-76871-61-2
ISBN-13: 978-76871-61-5

British Library Cataloguing-in-Publication Data
A catalogue record for this book is available from the British Library

Acknowledgements

Many people have contributed to the success of the Hague Expert Meetings, on which this book has been based.

We must particularly thank the Netherlands Foundation for Legal Research *NWO-SARO*, the Albeda Chair Trust *Stichting Albeda Leerstoel* and the Centre for Labour Relations in the Public Sector *CAOP*, for their moral and financial support, which enabled us to convene such a unique and select company of practicing mediators, academics, and representatives from both sides of industry as well as government.

We are particularly grateful to Mr Pieter van Aartsen, Mr Peter van der Geld and Ms Loes Spaans at CAOP, for their invaluable assistance during the Meetings, and to Ms Jacqueline Lensink, our publisher, for her continuous support and enthusiasm for the publication project.

We hope the book will canvas the fruitful relationships between those involved in the project and will find its way to further interested parties throughout Europe.

A.B, L.S., A.d.R., R.J., October 2006

CHAPTER I

Effective resolution of collective labour disputes in the public and private sector

Alex Brenninkmeijer and Loe Sprengers

1 Introduction

In October 1984, the *Advies- en Arbitragecommissie Rijksoverheid* (*AAC*) (Advisory and Arbitration Committee for the Central Public Sector), was installed. The task of this committee is to give advice or to arbitrate in collective labour disputes in certain parts of the Dutch public sector. There is also another similar committee for the local public sectors, the *LAAC*. For the private sector, there is no such institutionalized provision for solving collective labour disputes in the Netherlands.

On the occasion of the 20th anniversary of the *AAC*, we organized together with Annie de Roo and Rob Jagtenberg an expert meeting to discuss the function of the *AAC* in public labour relations in Holland. The question was raised as to how to explain the differences in the developments in the public and the private sector. The national expert meeting was a kick-off meeting for an international expert meeting that took place on 3 June 2005. The outcome of the national expert meeting was used for the development of a questionnaire that was sent to experts in the field of resolution of collective labour disputes in several EU Member States.

The aim of this international expert meeting was firstly to get more information about the way collective labour disputes are resolved in several EU Member States as well as the developments on the EU-level. Secondly, the aim was to inventory the conditions for the effective resolution of collective employment disputes. The participants of the expert meeting are engaged with the issue of resolving collective labour disputes at a scientific level or as mediators or conciliators. In this book you will find the results of this international expert meeting.

In the first chapter, we describe the developments in the Netherlands in the field of the resolution of collective labour disputes and conclude with a summary of the questionnaire that was sent to the participants of the international expert meeting and is the basis of the contribution of the experts.

In the next chapter, you will find the synthesis report of the national reports and the plenary discussions by Annie de Roo and Rob Jagtenberg. After that there is first a report on the EU perspective followed by the national reports.

2 Resolving of collective labour disputes in the Netherlands

a. The private sector

At present in the Netherlands, there is no institutionalized system of collective labour disputes settlement for the private sector, which is contrary to the civil sector as mentioned before.

This has not always been the case. In the 19th century, the *Kamers van Arbeid* (Labour Chambers) were the first statutory institutions responsible for labour dispute settlement in the Netherlands.[1] The *Kamers van Arbeid* were composed of an equal representation of employers and workers. Apart form their responsibility to prevent and to settle disputes, they had an advisory task concerning all labour matters. Joint boards established through the private initiative of employers and unions were not large in number and were not considered to function satisfactorily. Settlements reached through conciliation in the *Kamers van Arbeid* were not legally binding. Often the secretary of the *Kamers van Arbeid* was a practicing lawyer. The position of the secretary was financed by the government. He played an increasingly important role as an intermediary in conciliations.

In the early 1920s, there was widespread dissatisfaction with the *Kamers van Arbeid*. The government was interested in having institutions which could act more quickly and decidedly in the event of strikes. The idea of developing dispute settlement machinery jointly with both sides of industry was abandoned.

A new institution was introduced in 1923, the *Rijksbemiddelaar* (Government Mediator). It was a professional civil servant mediator, working alone.[2] The *Rijksbemiddelaar* had the responsibility to settle collective disputes, which were defined as disputes involving more than 50 workers. The *Rijksbemiddelaar* could intervene on his own motion. His services could also be requested by the mayors, or by the disputing parties themselves. In practice, the initiative to intervene was mostly taken by the *Rijksbemiddelaar* on his own motion or upon the request of the mayor. Employers and trade unions mistrusted the *Rijksbemiddelaar*. The institution was rendered inoperative during World War II and it was not re-activated after the war. Ever since, the Netherlands has done without permanent statutory machinery for the settlement of collective disputes in the private sector.

Since the late 1960s, both sides of industry have resisted the introduction of new statutory machinery for settling collective disputes.[3]

In 1969, the government proposed two bills.[4] The first, the bill on dispute settlement, provided for commissions of inquiry to be established whenever a strike was imminent. Strikes, whether imminent or already started, would have to be announced straightaway by any employer or employee involved to the president of the *SER* (Social Economic Council, the advisory tri-partite committee on social and economic issues of the government). If the strike was organized by a trade union, then the president of the *SER* would have to install a commission of inquiry. The members of the commission would be appointed from a list drafted by the Minister of Social Affairs in consultation with the *Stichting van de Arbeid* (a bipartite advisory committee). The task of the commission would be to collect

1 The Labour Chambers Act of 1897, withdrawn in 1922.

2 The Labour Disputes Act 1923.

3 A. de Roo and R. Jagtenberg, *Settling Labour Disputes in Europe*, Kluwer Law and Taxation Publishers: Deventer 1994, 262-263.

4 Bill 10.110 and Bill 10.111.

information about the circumstances leading to the strike and to do everything to avert a strike or to stop an on-going strike. The commission was, however, explicitly denied the power to arbitrate. It could act as a mediation board. It was free to take the initiative to mediate itself.

The second bill was introduced on instigation of the unions, who strongly criticized the court decisions rendered in 1958 and 1960. The bill provided that a strike would be deemed lawful, unless it would be contrary to a peace obligation in a collective agreement, or if certain rules had been ignored, or if a manifest disproportion existed between the object and consequences of the strike (lawful, unless...).

Both these bills were strongly criticized by employers' associations, trade unions and the *Stichting van de Arbeid*. The government then withdrew these proposed bills. Since then, no further legislative action has been taken on the subject.[5]

An important reason for the lack of new legislative initiatives are the developments in the case law. The principle of the 1969 proposed bill (strikes are lawful, unless...) has since 1972 been adopted in the court decisions. In 1986, in the most important decision of the *Hoge Raad* (Supreme Court) about the right to strike, the *Hoge Raad* recognized Article 6, section 4 European Social Charter (ESC) for the first time as the basis of the right to strike.[6] That is why the need for legislation decreased. The court decisions often fulfil an important role in an ongoing or starting strike. If the court decides the strike is forbidden, the unions respect that decision and stop the strike. If, on the other hand, the court decides the strike is lawful, most of the time the employers invite the unions for renewed negotiations and often in a short time an agreement is reached. In the last decade, it is frequently not the employer that asks the court to intervene in an ongoing strike, but a third party. This third party can be an interest group of consumers in the public health sector or in the public transport sector or companies that get in serious trouble with their own business because of the strike. This is usually the case with strikes that concern essential services. The case law has been characterized as allowing a strike for a short while, but not for too long, especially if it concerns essential services.[7]

This corresponds with the lack of a striking tradition in the Netherlands compared with other European countries. The percentage of union members in the working population, about 25%, can explain this as well as the nature of the Dutch people to be willing to reach an agreement by negotiating. As from the mid 1980s, employers' associations and trade unions in the Netherlands increasingly demonstrated a businesslike attitude and a willingness to reach agreement. It has been observed that this co-operative mood and practice of mutual

5 L. Tilstra, *Grenzen aan het stakingsrecht*, Kluwer: Deventer 1994, 24/25.

6 HR 30-5-1986, NJ 1986, 688.

7 L.C.J. Sprengers and R. v.d. Stege, 'Slechts een beetje staken mag? Het collectief actierecht ex art. 6 vierde lid en 31 ESH in de Nederlandse rechtspraktijk', *NJCM-Bulletin* 2004, 651-668.

consultation (the so-called *Polder Model*) has greatly contributed to restore the competitiveness of the Dutch industry in the 1980s and 1990s. From 2000, the drop in economic results and the presence of another coalition in power[8] after the elections in 2002, has put much pressure on the *Polder Model*. The willingness to come to an agreement between social partners and the government has decreased. The government seemed to prefer to go its own way on issues such as keeping elder employees longer on the job, changing the early retirement rules, diminishing the disability and unemployment payment, and the health insurance system. In November 2004, there was a large union demonstration in Amsterdam that was a signal for the government that the unions still were able to mobilize lots of people. It finally led to a new tripartite agreement on some of the major issues. In this period with a lot of changes in the social and economic policy of the government, the number of strikes was not higher than in the years before. This was probably because the unions realized that some measures were necessary for changing the economic position and for coping with the problem of the aging population along with the upcoming retirement of the baby-boomers.

In this climate, the social partners thus far felt no need to (re)introduce a permanent agency for settling disputes. It has been argued by many that the Netherlands does not need a settlement agency as the incidence of strikes is already extremely low.[9]

On the other hand, we can find an institutionalized way of dispute resolution in the *Wet op de ondernemingsraden (WOR)* (Works Council Act). All most all conflicts that concern the *WOR* have to be submitted for mediation to the *bedrijfscommissie* (joint sectoral committee).[10] The joint sectoral committees are composed of an equal representation of employers' organizations and unions within the sector. There are at this moment 24 *bedrijfscommissies*. The task of the *bedrijfscommissie* is first of all to mediate, and if that does not succeed to give a written report of its findings to the parties containing recommendations for settling the dispute. If the dispute has not been settled by then, it is possible to petition the sub-district *kantonrechter* (sub-district court judge). The *kantonrechter* can give a ruling that is binding on both parties. The legislator introduced

8 The centre-right cabinet Balkenende II with the Christian Democratic Party (CDA) and the two liberal parties, VVD and D'66. After three centre-left cabinets with the social democratic party, PvdA and the two liberal parties VVD and D'66. Between cabinets Kok III and Balkenende II, there was the unsuccessful cabinet Balkenende I, with the CDA, VVD and the LPF, the party of Pim Fortuijn, who was killed a few days before the elections in 2001.

9 Annie de Roo, 'Labour Conciliation, Mediation and Arbitration in the Netherlands', in: Fernando Valdés Dal-Ré (dir), *Labour Conciliation, Mediation and Arbitration in European Union Countries*, Ministerio de Trabajo y Asuntos Sociales, Espana 2003, 292.

10 Only for disputes concerning the right of advice of the works council there is the possibility of an appeal with the *Ondernemingskamer* (Enterprise section) of the *Gerechtshof* (Amsterdam Court of Appeal).

the *bedrijfscommissie* in the Works Council Act to filter the number of disputes that could be addressed to the *kantonrechter.*

The few figures that are available show that in only about 10% of the cases that are submitted to the *bedrijfscommissies* one of the parties actually starts the lawsuit by submitting a petition to the to the *kantonrechter.*[11] One could say that the *bedrijfscommissies* as a filter are effective. But there is also a lot of criticism on how the *bedrijfscommissies* function. The fact that one is obliged to submit a case to the *bedrijfscommissie* is criticized. It would be better to change it in a voluntary proceeding. Many *bedrijfscommissies* never see both parties. They give parties the opportunity to state the case in writing and then send a written report to both parties with recommendations. Sometimes the recommendation is that the *bedrijfscommissie* has come to the conclusion that both parties have a different view on the issue and it advises them to address the *kantonrechter.* In those cases the members of the *bedrijfscommissie* cannot come to a unanimous appraisal because of the different opinions between the employers and union-representatives in the *bedrijfscommissies.* For an effective mediation, it is necessary to talk to both parties and mediate between them. That is not possible if the whole proceeding is conducted in writing only.

In 2005 the legislator proposed a new law to change the Works Council Act, the *Wet Medezeggenschap Werknemers* (Law on determination of workers).[12] This proposal was heavily criticized and was withdrawn when it became clear there was not enough support in parliament. One of the proposals that hardly was criticized was the removal of the *bedrijfscommissies.* The possibility was given to the entrepreneur and the works council to come to an agreement about a voluntary committee for mediation or advice. It should also be possible to transform *bedrijfscommissies* by collective labour agreement into a voluntary mediation committee for all the companies that are tied by that collective labour agreement. In the proposed new law, the *SER* was asked to co-ordinate the change to voluntary mediation committee(s).

At the moment, the discussion about the future of the Works Council Act is starting over from the beginning. It will take a while before it is clear if and in what way the Works Council Act can or will be changed. The possibility that changes will be made in the mandatory mediation procedure by the *bedrijfscommissies* is considerable.

b. The public sector

In the 1980s, a process began to standardize labour relations in the public sector – a process to bring public sector labour relations more in line with those customary in the private sector. As a result of this process central,

---

11 J.C.M. van Horne, *In het voorportaal van de rechter,* SDU: Den Haag 1997, 105; L.C.J. Sprengers, *Collectieve belangen- uiteenlopende conflicten,* SDU: Den Haag 2003, 102.

12 Wetsontwerp (Draft bill) 29 818.

local and functional government authorities have become increasingly important as employers. Before the 1980s, the most important labour conditions of all civil servants followed the outcome of the negotiations at a central level between the Ministry of Domestic Affairs and the unions. The need for more flexibility and the differences between the various sectors within the public sector itself led to the *Sectorenmodel* (Sectoral Model). At first eight sectors were created: central government, several local authorities, the police, the army, the judges, the universities and education. At the moment there are 13 sectors. In each sector the employers and the unions negotiate separately to come to an agreement about the labour conditions for the civil servants in the sector. To secure a more equal position in the negotiations between public employers and the union, the *overeenstemmingsvereiste* (requirement to agree) is introduced. A public-employer cannot make a change in a rule that concerns the rights or duties of civil servants unless he has reached an agreement with the civil servants' unions. There are four different unions that represent the civil servants. An agreement is reached if a majority of the unions agrees. If there is a draw between the unions, the decision is up to the employer to decide whether there is an agreement or not.[13]

One of the reasons the *overeenstemmingsvereiste* was introduced was the special positions of civil servants on the issue of the right to strike. The Dutch government made an exception by the ratification of the ESC in 1980 in Article 6 section 4 for the civil servants. In expectation of a special bill on the right to strike for civil servants, the exception was made. The ratification of the ESC took place in 1980, after having signed the charter in 1961. The reason it took so long was that before ratification, the ban on strikes for civil servants in the penal laws had to be removed.

In 1980 a government commission came up with two draft bills: one about the resolution of collective disputes in the public sector and the other about the right to strike for civil servants.[14] In that last draft bill, it was proposed to also recognize the right to strike as mentioned in Article 6 section 4 ESC for civil servants. Excluded were those jobs that unambiguously constitute a danger for the in Article 31 ESC mentioned values if they are not fulfilled, such as the police and the army. The draft bill also made it possible for the Minister of Domestic Affairs to forbid a strike. In the years that followed, several different draft bills were proposed and discussed by different cabinets, but none of them received enough support.

In 1983 there were huge conflicts in the public sector about a proposal of the government to cut the wages of the civil servants. As a result thereof, many strikes were organized by the unions of the civil servants. In 11 cases, different courts were asked to forbid an ongoing strike.[15] In all those cases, the principle

---

[13] L.C.J. Sprengers, 'Hfst 7 Collectief Overleg en Conflict', in: E. Verhulp (red.): *Inleiding Nederlands Ambtenarenrecht*, BJU: Den Haag 2005.

[14] Rapport Commissie Toxopeus II 1980.

[15] A.P.H.C.M. Jaspers, *De ambtenarenstakingen, grenzen in kort geding*, Kluwer: Deventer 1983.

of the right to strike for civil servants was recognized, although there still was not a bill as announced, and there was the exception made by the ratification of the ESC. In the judgments, it was made clear that due to the view of law, the civil servants in the Netherlands also had the right to strike, but often with certain restrictions. Afterwards in other cases, the *Hoge Raad* confirmed the principle of the right to strike for civil servants.[16]

These developments in the case law were the main reason that the need for a bill on the right to strike for civil servants decreased. Recently the exception made by the ratification of the ESC is changed. The exception only remains for the civil servants in the army sector.

The other draft bill about the resolution of collective disputes in the public sector from 1980 made a difference between the advice that could be asked in each case of a third party. Arbitration is only possible by the law established arbitration committee. It was the outcome of the Article 6 section 3 ESC imposed duty to the government to realize procedures for the resolution of collective labour disputes, though only for the public sector. Although this bill has never been accepted, it formed the basis of the later established *Advies- en Arbitrage-commissies* (Advisory and Arbitration Committee). In every public sector, the employers and union have made rulings about how to proceed when it is not possible to come to an agreement on issues that concern the *overeenstemmings-vereiste*. There are two committees: one for the sectors: central government, police, army, judges and education, the *AAC*. The other one is for the local government sectors, the *LAAC*.

The *AAC* started in 1984. In the first twenty years, the *AAC* was called in 79 times. That is an average of 4 cases a year ranging from zero to a maximum of 8 cases a year. Most disputes came from the sectors of education and the police. In 46 cases, the *AAC* gave an advice. Most of the time the parties followed this advice. In 10 cases the *AAC* was asked to arbitrate. The other cases were withdrawn before an advice was given.

In the first years of its existence, the *AAC* had an important function to set the rules for free and open negotiations between the public employers and the unions. In particular, the central government had to learn to distinguish its two roles: the role of the government and the role of the employer. The *AAC* is of the opinion that the government in the role of employer cannot dictate the outcome of the negotiations with the unions just by referring to the policy of the government about, for example, the development of wages in general and social security benefits. An important mark of equal and open labour negotiations is that both parties should be prepared to listen to each other's arguments and seriously try to reach an agreement.

At the moment, it is discussed whether the process of standardization of the labour relations in the public sector towards the private sector should culminate in a uniform labour law for both the civil and the public sector. In September

---

16 HR 30-5-1986, NJ 1986, 688; HR 11-12-1992, NJ 1996, 229.

2005, a governmental advisory committee advised that it could be done. The advantages are less regulation and more flexibility. As an important disadvantage was mentioned the high costs of the huge legislative operation that will be needed.[17] For a small part of the public sector, there should remain a different system.

In October 2005, the Albeda Foundation organized the first public debate on this issue.[18] The cabinet plans to bring out its vision about the future of the civil servants at the end of 2006.

This makes the issue in which way effective resolution of collective labour disputes in the public and private sector should take place in the Netherlands very relevant. If the standardization will be finalised by creating a uniform labour law, one of the issues will then be whether there should be an institutionalized provision for solving collective labour disputes, such as the *AAC* for the public sector, or no institutionalized provision, such as is the case at present in the market sector? Or is another way of resolution of collective labour disputes preferable?

3 Questionnaire

This brings us to the questionnaire.[19] In the questionnaire, we asked the experts from several EU-countries to give more information about the facilities that are provided, by the state or both sides of industry, for assisting parties in resolving collective labour disputes. We were interested in the working of these facilities. To what extent do they satisfy a distinct need? Are there differences between the public and private sector? How are these facilities financed?

In case the facilities have been institutionalized, we wanted to know whether the institutionalization has contributed to a gain or a loss in time for the handling of (imminent) disputes. Has it amounted to a restriction of the right to strike? We were furthermore interested whether the institutionalization of mediation as a remedial intervention technique has contributed to the prevention of disputes.

We asked about the role of the mediator in the process of settling collective labour disputes. How important is it that the mediator has branch-specific knowledge? How many staff are involved with mediation?

Another issue was how the requirements set by Article 6, section 3 ESC should be met. Are there particular insights in the area of dispute resolutions and/or collective bargaining that could have relevance for, in particular, the new EU-members?

---

17 Interdepartementaal Beleidsonderzoek 2004-2005, No. 6, 'Buitengewoon normaal".

18 L.C.J. Sprengers (ed), *Heeft de ambtelijke status nog toekomst?*, Publicatiereeks Overheid & Arbeid 2005-18, CAOP: Den Haag 2005.

19 The questionnaire has been included on p. 162 of this volume.

Against the backdrop of emerging EU collective agreements and genuine European companies, we asked the experts what would be the best way to deal with cross-border collective labour disputes in the nearby future. In particular, we were interested in the lesson to be learned from the experiences in other countries for the Dutch case.

All these issues and many more were discussed during the expert meeting in June 2005 in The Hague. In the next chapter, in the synthesis report, some conclusions will be drawn from the national reports and the discussion. The focus will be on the lessons to be learned form the experiences in other countries as well as lessons to be learned for an effective resolution of collective employment disputes in general. Also, any advice in general for dealing with collective labour conflicts in a way that contributes to prevention or managing those conflicts will be discussed.

CHAPTER 2

Effective resolution of collective labour disputes

A synthesis of national reports and plenary discussions

Annie de Roo and Rob Jagtenberg

1 Introduction

In this chapter, an effort is made to provide a synthesis analysis of the National Reports presented during the expert meeting in The Hague on 3 June 2005. This is a formidable task, in view of the wealth of ideas and materials that came to the fore, not only in the Reports, but also in the ensuing discussions. These discussions followed various themes. Some themes were derived from the questionnaire, sent to the national rapporteurs in preparation of the expert meeting. Additional themes were formulated on the spot, following the presentations. We have chosen to structure this analysis around both the questionnaire and the newly formulated themes. Thereby, we have sought to integrate a number of the – originally – twelve questions in the questionnaire into 4 or 5 wider themes. With the additional themes included, in the end 9 themes in all remain, around which this analysis can be organized.[1]

It will be impossible to do justice to all speakers and discussants in this synthesis report which – by its very nature – must be selective.

In addition, with the benefit of hindsight, we have chosen to occasionally expand beyond the actual discussions, where we felt that important underlying, or complementary, developments have remained underexposed but yet need to be clarified.

2 Fruitful comparison

The first theme emerged during the discussions and concerns some preliminary requirements for fruitful comparison.

Two aspects of comparison need to be mentioned here, that is 1) the way dispute resolution methods are defined and 2) the wider context of the industrial relations system. First, how are the very concepts of 'conciliation', 'mediation' and other modes of dispute resolution defined nationally? Do we need a common terminology if we are to have a genuine European discussion?

The meaning of dispute resolution concepts is often country-specific and, sometimes within one and the same country, area-specific. Thus, in England and Spain, 'conciliation' (in labour relations) refers to a lesser degree of third party involvement (*i.e.* acting as a mere go-between) than the concept of 'mediation' (which implies the neutral formulating proposals for a solution). In other countries, such as Germany, the meaning of these two concepts is exactly the other way around, with conciliation normally being understood as denoting *Schlichtung*.

Yet other countries do not differentiate at all between conciliation and mediation, or utilize concepts that have connotations unique to that country. The concept of *mirenje* in Servo-Croatian could serve as just one example here.

1 See for the full text of the original questionnaire p. 162 of this volume.

For the purpose of this chapter, we will use the concepts of conciliation and mediation interchangeably. It should be noted that the focus of both the national reports and the discussions was on conciliation and mediation: methods based on negotiation and negotiated solutions. By contrast, arbitration, as a method based on imposed decisions, was not really addressed.[2]

Particular modes of dispute resolution may be related exclusively to particular types of labour disputes, and it was generally acknowledged that the well-known distinction between disputes over interests and disputes over rights, and collective versus individual disputes (resulting in essentially a four-cell block of dispute categories) may still prove to be useful for the present debate. There was general support to confine the discussions primarily to collective disputes over interests.

This observation brought the participants to underscore the importance of the wider context of the industrial relations system in which dispute resolution mechanisms are embedded. Here lies the second focal point of comparative analysis.[3]

It is arguably the unique path of development of any nation's industrial relations system that will determine whether the outlook of dispute resolution is more 'tri-partite' or more 'bi-partite in outlook', when and how a neutral is to become involved and what the desired qualifications of this neutral should be.

Reference could also be made to the 2002 synthesis report by Fernando Valdés Dal-Ré, who pointed out that the status of conciliation and mediation can best be examined by taking into account two other elements of any nation's industrial and legal system: first, the presence (or absence) of a tradition of collective bargaining, and second the confidence put in the judicial system.[4] Thus, the two extremes on the curve of dispute resolution techniques (*i.e.* bilateral negotiation, and imposed court decisions) should also be analyzed in order to assess the intermediate modes of conciliation/mediation properly.

In his synthesis report, Valdés Dal-Ré made another important observation: historically, different European countries could be easily plotted on different positions along this dispute resolution curve – with some countries, such as France, Spain and Greece traditionally being more 'interventionist' emphasiz-

---

2 Reference is made to an earlier synthesis report on collective labour disputes, drafted for a European Commission sponsored conference: Antoine Jacobs, *The Resolution of Industrial Disputes*, Labour Relations Commission: Dublin, 1993. Professor Jacobs indicated at page II/8 of his report, that "[...] in the majority of European countries voluntary arbitration has little significance in the settlement of collective disputes, be they about rights or about interests".

3 A more detailed analysis is provided by, inter alia, R. Bean, *Comparative Industrial Relations, an Introduction to Cross-national Perspectives*, Routledge: London/Sydney 1985.

4 F. Valdés Dal-Ré, *Labour Conciliation, Mediation and Arbitration in European Union Countries*, Ministerio de Trabajo y Asuntos Sociales: Madrid 2003, 29 ff.

ing legal regulation and judicial dispute resolution, and other countries (such as England) being more 'abstentionist', favouring collective bargaining, preferably without any judicial intervention. The reality of today, however, shows that traditions are not to stay forever, and that *e.g.* interventionist countries are moving towards more abstentionist positions now.[5]

Today's process of globalization provides a further incentive to convergence, where bargaining (and hence dispute resolution) is increasingly decentralized to plant level, while at the same time increasingly assuming transnational dimensions. It seems we are witnessing the beginning of a quarter turn rotation of (formerly) 'national' industrial relations systems, towards multiple settings of transnational bargaining within business conglomerates operating globally, or Europe-wide.

This common development makes it all the more relevant to convene and compare national expertise in labour dispute resolution, not only for the sake of the Netherlands taking cognizance of its neighbours, but for all European members, to re-align the 'family ties'.

During the expert meeting it became increasingly clear that the impact of the globalization process on dispute resolution techniques requires more attention. Notably what springs to mind is the emerging 'partnership-approach'. As William Brown puts it: "The scope for confrontational bargaining is drastically reduced by the internationalisation of the world's economy. [...] Owners can increasingly wander the world, choosing the labour cost structures that suit them best; and these tend to suit established trade unions least".[6]

These issues will be addressed more extensively *infra*, as themes 5, 6 and 7. First, however, some themes from the questionnaire need to be highlighted.

3 Public versus private sector (facilities)?

We will take together questions 1 and 4, and 2, 3 and 11 from the questionnaire for the second theme: differences between the public and private sector, and the dispute resolution facilities provided for each of these sectors respectively.

Despite indications that differences between the public and private sector become less and less accentuated across Europe, a bird's eye view suggests that differences continue to exist between the countries represented at the expert meeting, as to the precise delineation of the category of public officers (civil or crown servants, *Beamten*, *Ambtenaren*), as opposed to those employed under a

5 F. Valdés Dal-Ré, *o.c.*, 43.

6 W. Brown, 'Third Party Labour Market Intervention in Open Economies', in: J.E. Isaac and R.D. Lansbury (eds.), *The Deregulation of the Australian Labour Market: Essays in Honour of Keith Hancock*, London/Sydney 2005.

'regular' contract (whether by a government agency, or in the market sector).[7] It may be helpful at this point to refer to the *Pellegrin* v *France* case, in which the European Court of Human Rights introduced an autonomous European definition of 'civil servants', interestingly by reference to the EC Treaty (a striking example of Council of Europe and European Community synergy).[8] On the whole, the pattern that appears is that distinctions between the status of public officers and those employed under contracts have mostly disappeared (*e.g.* in respect of the right to join a union). A possible exception remains where for certain categories of public officers, particularly those acting as depositaries of state authority, such as the armed forces, the police and the prison service, the right to strike may still be subject to limitations which differ from country to country.[9]

A common pattern is that today, by far, the largest number of strikes appears to take place within those sectors that are directly or indirectly funded by the state, hence the (semi-) public sector. An explanation for this common pattern has been furnished by William Brown. Using again his argument of exposure to world competition, Brown observes that for public sector trade unions "[...] membership has generally remained high relative to private enterprise" [...], and that with public sector monopolies the picture is not quite so bleak" – though deteriorating in view of the tendency to privatization and outsourcing.[10]

The question of whether dispute resolution facilities differ for the public and private sector respectively gave rise to roughly three categories of answers. First, in most countries represented, the facilities available are equally used in the public and private sector. Second, there are those countries (notably Belgium and Spain) where facilities are available for the private sector but not for the public sector. Thirdly, there is the Netherlands, where the reverse is true.

It seems logical that, where the differences between both sectors are increasingly on the wane, dispute resolution mechanisms are equally available for both sectors. The explanation furnished for the situation in Belgium and Spain is that both countries have followed the French model of strict separation of the service public including the entire domain of legal instruments to which state agencies are a party. This explanation deserves further research, and perhaps in the future other countries, notably France itself, should be included into the comparison.

---

7 "Employees' collective rights in the public sector" was one of the conference themes at the 14th World Conference on Comparative Law, held in Athens, 1994. Various national rapporteurs identified a process of 'normalization' unfolding in the public sector. See for instance E. Hondius (Ed.), *Netherlands Reports to the 14th International Congress of Comparative Law*, T.M.C. Asser Institute: The Hague 1994, 191 ff.

8 European Court of Human Rights, 8 December 1999, *Pellegrin* v. *France*, Application 28541/95.

9 Reference is made to the various national reports incorporated in this book, for instance the differences between the situation in Finland and Sweden. A further informative document on the UK is Susan Corby, *Public Sector Disputes and Third Party Intervention*, Acas research paper 02/03, London 2003.

10 Brown *o.c.*, 4.

The situation in the Netherlands remains exceptional, not so much for the presence of a public sector facility (which has been created *inter alia* to help the unions and the government in its role as an employer to develop a habitus of bargaining, similar to the private sector), but rather for the absence of any facility in the private sector. It has been suggested by the present authors that this position may be explained from the exceptionally lengthy period (more than 30 years) of Dutch post-war governmental interventionism, notably a dirigist wage policy.[11]

This leads us to the issue of the nature of the facilities provided in the countries concerned. Permanent agencies can be found in all countries, but differences exist in the way these facilities are organized and funded, the way they are staffed, their coverage of the industrial relations landscape, and the extent to which they are actually used. State-funded facilities can be found in all countries except Germany and the Netherlands' private sector.

In some countries (*Sociaal Bemiddelaars*, Belgium, National Conciliator's Office, Finland), these facilities have been integrated into the state administrative machinery, whereas in others, the facilities have been accommodated in separate entities (Acas, United Kingdom, *Medlingsinstitutet*, Sweden, *AAC*, the Netherlands), whereas in yet another country, (*SIMA*, Spain) the facilities have been created privately, although subsidized through public funds.[12]

In Germany, *Schlichtungsstelle* (conciliation committees) created on the basis of collective agreements are widespread, and these committees are essentially funded by the social partners themselves.[13] In the Dutch private sector, a number of such committees also exist, although their coverage seems considerably lower than their German counterparts.[14]

National statistics (where available) suggest that in most countries the facilities do meet a distinct demand, in that their services are regularly sought.[15]

A related aspect, that was not discussed but must be mentioned here, is the problem inherent in measuring the 'success' of any dispute resolution facility. A preliminary question is whether the referral to such facilities is voluntary or compulsory. That issue will be addressed briefly hereafter, under the next

11 A. de Roo and R. Jagtenberg, 'Europa in de polder', in: *Tijdschrift voor Mediation*, No. 4, 2005.

12 The statutory machinery based on the *Kontrollratsgesetz* is, compared to conciliation proceedings in collective agreements, virtually a dead letter, according to the German rapporteur.

13 P.F. van der Heijden, *Een eerlijk proces in het sociaal recht?*, Kluwer: Deventer 1984. But then, in the Netherlands there had not been an event similar to the *Margarethenhof* Agreement in Germany.

14 For *SIMA* data, reference is made to Maria Luz Rodriguez Fernández, 'Labour Conciliation, Mediation and Arbitration in Spain', in: F. Valdés Dal-Ré, *o.c.*, 357, and for Belgium to E. Delattre, 'Labour Conciliation, Mediation and Arbitration in Belgium', in: F. Valdés dal Ré, 84. For Sweden, Finland and the UK the reader is referred to the national reports incorporated in this book, and in addition to the Acas annual reports which can be downloaded from the internet – www.acas.org.uk.

15 W. Felstiner, R.L. Abel and A. Sarat, 'The Emergence and Transformation of Disputes: Naming, Blaming, Claiming', in: *Law & Society Review* 1980, No. 15.

theme (Article 6 of the European Social Charter). More complicated to assess is the number of (voluntary) applications to such facilities measured against the potential baseline of emerging disputes.[16] Only if that information were available, could one begin to assess the effectiveness of such facilities in terms of their contribution to industrial peace and economic stability. Even then it might be difficult to solve the well-known imbroglio of how the presence or absence of a facility relates to the incidence of industrial action, and whether the investment in such a facility would soon be earned back.[17] Just the same, it is often purported that in the analogous case of a fire, one cannot evaluate the mere availability of fire extinguisher equipment on the basis of a straightforward cost-benefit analysis.[18]

The number of mediators/conciliators varies from country to country, from just one full-timer and some part-timers in Finland to a few dozen (usually part-time *Bemiddelaars* and part-time chairpersons to joint committees) in Belgium to approximately 50 full-time collective conciliators with Acas in the United Kingdom. The 30 or so mediators in Sweden's *Mediation Institutet* are not employed, but paid per assignment, and the same applies to the mediators appointed from *SIMA's* list – in both cases honoraria are paid to the account of the state budget.

Although it might be tempting to compare the number of disputes to the (re-calculated) amount of full-time equivalent invested per country, such a comparison would be misguiding and even dangerous, as multiple intermediate factors will co-determine the flow and complexity of cases in each country differently.[19]

No clear pattern emerged with regard to the professional requirements and background of mediators. In some countries (the *Sociaal Bemiddelaars* in Belgium and Acas in the United Kingdom), branch-specific knowledge is certainly valued and even encouraged through the career structures within the relevant organizations providing mediation. The Belgian mediators, for example, have all been assigned a specific area of industry through the linkage with the joint committee.

Elsewhere, branch-specific knowledge is implied by the nature of the facility (the *Schlichtungsabkommen* in Germany). However, even in these countries, experience in handling disputes and seniority seem to play an equally important role. In other countries, such as Spain, the emphasis is more on affinity with

16 The metaphor is borrowed from A.T.J.M. Jacobs, 'Onderzoek, verzoening, bemiddeling', in: *Ibid., Blinde vlekken in het sociaal recht, Liber amicorum Prof. B.S. Frenkel*, Kluwer: Deventer 1986.

17 For a discussion of similar methodological problems in the international comparison of the efficiency of courts in adjudicating disputes, see J. Blank et al., *Bench Marking in an International Perspective*, Ecorys: Rotterdam 2004.

18 For a discussion of the Committee of Independent Experts' view on Art. 6 section 3 of the Charter, see Annie de Roo and Rob Jagtenberg, *Settling Labour Disputes in Europe*, Kluwer: Deventer/Boston 1994, 352 ff.

19 M. Luz Rodriguez Fernandez, in: F. Valdés Dal-Ré, *o.c.*, 333-335.

labour relations generally (*SIMA*), whereas in Sweden the crucial quality is said to be the mediator's experience of previous negotiations and their ability to find solutions to difficult problems.

4 European Social Charter requirements

A third theme emanated from the questionnaire again, through combining questions 10, 4 and 6: how should the requirements of Article 6 section 3 of the European Social Charter be met? Must mediation facilities be 'institutionalized', and, if so, would not this restrict the right to strike, laid down in section 4 of the same Charter Article?

Some confusion arose as to the proper meaning of the word 'institutionalization'. This concept can either refer to the mediation facility and its staff, or to the procedure for referring imminent disputes to mediation.

As far as the facility itself is concerned, it should be pointed out that neither the wording of Article 6, nor the explanations by the Committee of Independent Experts of the Council of Europe are crystal-clear. Section 3 stipulates that the "Contracting Parties undertake [...] to promote the establishment and use of appropriate machinery for conciliation [...]".

The Committee of Independent Experts made it clear that conciliation is to be understood as a mere facility to secure both parties' right to bargain collectively, hence conciliation is meant to be facilitative.[20] As to the basis and format of the conciliation machinery, the Committee indicated that the appropriate machinery may be established by legislation, collective agreement or industrial practice. So the very act of establishment is not necessarily performed by the state. However, the state should 'promote'. Does this imply for instance some degree of public funding of the facility? It has been argued elsewhere that some of the facilities under discussion at the Hague Expert Meeting would probably not function if they could not be accessed free of charge.[21]

During the expert meeting, the nature of Article 6 of the Charter as a potential legal obligation on state parties remained unresolved. It can be added that, elsewhere, we have argued that from the Committee's reports it can be inferred that Article 6 does confer a duty upon the state parties to monitor the efficacy of such conciliation machinery, even if it is established by the social partners themselves.[22]

In this respect, for example, the present situation in the Netherlands' private sector, where conciliation committees established by collective agreements only seem to have limited coverage, may give rise to some concern. In the meantime, the Dutch social partners do from time to time appoint *ad hoc* mediators. A

---

20 A. de Roo and R. Jagtenberg, *o.c.*, 354.

21 Both German and Dutch case law bear witness to these tests.

22 A.de Roo and R. Jagtenberg, *Europese Mediationpraktijken*, BJU: Den Haag 2004, 99.

major advantage of *ad hoc* mediation, thus indicated the Dutch employers' representative, is that the parties can appoint a mediator based on their own terms of reference. Before getting to the referral issue, we hope it may have become clear that institutionalization of the facility does not necessarily imply a prestigious office building populated by government employed mediators. What counts is the efficacy of mediation. Efficacy, however, may be related to some degree of permanency and professionalism. We will revert to this aspect under the next theme of this synthesis report.

Institutionalization of the referral of disputes to mediation brings the right to strike issue into focus.

What became clear from the reports and the discussion at this point is that the mediation schemes discussed were essentially voluntary; although at closer inspection, some mechanisms amount to a strong incentive to resort to such mediation schemes and to make an effort at reconciliation, before industrial action can legitimately be called for.

In several countries, courts will apply a proportionality (or ultimum remedium) test to industrial action, which will encompass a review of the efforts made to find an amicable solution.[23]

Sweden poses an interesting case in that the Mediation Institutet was primarily introduced to promote an efficient wage formation process, *inter alia* by stimulating the social partners to develop timetables for negotiations. An incentive provided thereto (by the legislator) is that parties calling for industrial action would have to refer their dispute compulsorily to the institute unless they had concluded an agreement on negotiation, including (registered) time schedules. In that case, the parties would be exempted from compulsory mediation – and it would henceforth be entirely up to the parties to apply to the institute voluntarily. In view of the number of agreements on negotiation concluded thus far, this incentive seems to have worked well, meaning that for the bigger part of the industrial relations system, mediation has become a voluntary option.

In the United Kingdom, where involvement of Acas may have been written into a large number of (non binding) collective agreements, there are effectively no restrictions on the right to strike ensuing from participation in a mediation effort. Restrictions rather follow from procedural rules pertaining to the conduct of strike ballots.

An interesting issue raised was whether the social partners do not give their right to negotiate directly (using their own strategy) away, if they are put under some pressure to resort to mediation.

The British rapporteur, drawing from his multi-annual experience, pointed out that Acas essentially 'waits outside the room' until it is called in by the social partners themselves, usually after they have ended up in a stalemate.

---

[23] Department of Trade and Industry: *Routes to Resolution, Improving Dispute Resolution in Britain*, London 2002. Various in-depth advisory programmes are reported in the Acas Annual Reports.

Mediation practice shows that stalemates mostly arise when the discourse has become too personalized. A shared experience is that, increasingly, managers seem to lack the necessary negotiation skills and the right attitude. It seems that they suffer from 'macho-management'. Also unions demonstrate a lack of skills. Instead of building up bargaining expertise striking wage deals, union negotiators are increasingly taken up by presenting individual rights issues at tribunals.

This issue of 'loss of skills' will be addressed in more detail hereafter, under themes 6 and 8. The conclusion thus far is, in the wordings of the British rapporteur that mediation does not cut across tactical negotiation: rather, there is a need to intervene when things have become too personalized.

5 Institutionalization and prevention

The next theme concerns the issue of whether institutionalized mediation – that is: established facilities of a permanent character and therefore readily accessible to disputants – contributes to swift handling, or even prevention, of disputes (questions 5 and 7 from the questionnaire). The issue of branch-specific knowledge (question 8) is also touched upon.

Of the corresponding questions in the questionnaire, the one pertaining to the prevention of disputes was arguably the easiest to answer. The question was inspired by the well-known potential of novel mediation techniques to explore the real causes underlying a single – or a whole series – of disputes. The expected linkage between some form of permanency and professionalism on the one hand, and the potential to take away the cause for not only present but also future disputes on the other, was inspired by a comparative European survey into the practice of court annexed mediation (though not exclusively in the area of employment disputes). This survey had demonstrated that mediation providers, which had become well rooted in society and had come to enjoy the confidence of large segments of potential users, also had the best prospects for deploying novel mediation techniques successfully.[24]

The existence of the 'permanency-professionalism-preventive potential' linkage was broadly confirmed by the Acas experience.

Here, collective conciliators always look into underlying problems and move on from mere conciliation into in-depth advisory projects, where deeper causes are suspected. The 'A 'of 'Advisory' does not come first in the Acas acronym without reason. A recent Department of Trade and Industry survey confirms that, due to its permanent status and professionalism, Acas – building upon at least 30 years of experience – has come to enjoy the confidence of both sides of industry, for conciliation/mediation as well as for its in-depth advisory work.[25]

---

[24] R. Jagtenberg and A. de Roo, 'Mediation in het bedrijfsleven', in: *Justitiële Verkenningen*, 2000, No. 9, 54 ff.

[25] Observation made by the attending Dutch expert professor Asscher-Vonk.

Further confirmation of the linkage between institutionalization and prevention came from Belgium, and to some extent from Germany.

In Belgium, the prevention of disputes is explicitly written into the charter of the *Sociaal Bemiddelaars*, next to the (curative) mediation of disputes arisen already. This task of prevention is facilitated by the dense network of professional contacts of the *Bemiddelaar*, inter alia with the Labour Inspectorate.

The German rapporteur drew attention to a mediation facility in Germany that is perhaps more strongly institutionalized than the agreement-based Schlichtungsabkommen, *i.e.* the statutory based tripartite conciliation committees (*Einigungsstelle*) within companies, charged with mediating (and eventually deciding) disputes between management and works council. These conciliation committees are on the whole quite active and successful, as they are composed of staff (management and workers) employed at the plant itself. Due to the familiarity with the underlying causes of problems in their immediate vicinity, these conciliation committees can often solve problems swiftly, and – where relevant – prevent further disputes from arising, by addressing the real causes.

Interestingly, this proximity and familiarity factor was also acknowledged in the Netherlands recently, at the national Mediation Day conference 2005. Here, various spokesmen from leading Dutch industries indicated that in order for mediation to become an accepted option, it will be essential for the companies to know the mediator, and more specifically, to be certain that the mediator knows the company. These views confirmed the findings of an earlier survey by the present authors among in-house lawyers in four branches of industry.[26]

Likewise, the on-going debate about the role of the Dutch *bedrijfscommissies* seems to confirm this picture. These commissions are the statutory mediation committees that have to be involved in disputes between the employer and the works council, as a preliminary step before an application to court can be made. The widespread dissatisfaction with these committees seems to spring from their rather detached position.[27]

Although the emerging picture is not entirely unequivocal – see the final paragraph under theme 2 *supra* – it appears that branch-specific knowledge does play a certain role when it comes to the acceptance and credibility of mediators.

The issue of mediation tied to the works councils reminds us that, next to mediation in traditional collective bargaining disputes, the role of mediation facilities at this level deserve more attention. The common European trend towards decentralization in industrial relations provides an all the more compelling reason to do so (see hereinafter, theme 6).

---

[26] The Employment Act 2002 (Dispute Resolution) Regulations 2004 require employers to have proper grievance procedures in place for employees to resort to, prior to applying to court. Examples of recent Belgian court-annexed mediation initiatives are to be found in the Belgian national report.

[27] For a comparative overview see J. Visser, *Industrial Relations in Europe 2004*, report to the European Commission, chapter 1.

Whether or not institutionalized mediation generally contributes to a swifter handling of (imminent) disputes, and hence a gain in time compared to *ad hoc* mediation, is a question that could not be answered during this expert meeting. Obviously, this question necessitates a comparative analysis of both *ad hoc* and institutional mediations. The subject looks interesting, but has to be stalled on the (European?) research agenda for the time being.

6 Changes in collective bargaining and in-court adjudication

We now return to the impact of globalization, starting out with the discussions on the changing industrial relations systems in Europe, the very environment of dispute resolution facilities.

As was pointed out *supra*, mediation facilities can be regarded as the middle piece of a triptych, with collective bargaining at the one extreme, and the judicial system at the other. The nature of the relationship of mediation to both extremes could perhaps best be characterized as a substitution effect relationship: when collective bargaining is not well developed, mediation needs to step in, in order to get parties back on track and, where necessary, as an aid to instil in the social partners a habitus of working together. At the other extreme, where the judicial system does not function properly or is distrusted, mediation will be resorted to as a reasonable alternative to (if not the primary choice of) settlement.

In other words: the less one can rely on one of the methods at the extremes, the more popular (or necessary) mediation facilities may get. During the expert meeting, this relationship was not discussed as explicitly as in the literature concerned, but it may be helpful to reproduce this framework in this synthesis report.

The reason will be clear: there was general consensus that, as a consequence of globalization, dramatic changes are taking place at both extremes.

First, as to thc judicial system: the courts constitute an integral part of the public sector, which is now increasingly pressurized in all developed economies. The need to contain court budgets and to maximize efficiency in the administration of justice undoubtedly forms one of the main drives behind the promotion of court annexed mediation programmes throughout Europe – that is, next to more idealistic motives such as 'individualized justice' and 'empowerment' of disputants.

As a consequence, courts are increasingly scrutinizing incoming cases. This tendency is probably most visible in the United Kingdom, in the handling of individual employment disputes by the employment tribunals.[28] From here,

[28] B. Keller, *Industrial Relations and European Integration: Trans- and Supranational Developments and Prospects*, Ahsgate: London 2003.

pressure is thus building up to revert disputes back to the workplace, to have at least those issues solved there that can be solved there.

A spin-off of this development of court-annexed mediation is increasing familiarity among the population at large with mediation as a mode of dispute resolution.

Second, the role and character of collective bargaining is gradually changing throughout Europe. With the noticeable exception of the Scandinavian countries, the extent of trade union affiliation has dropped everywhere, in the United Kingdom for example from more than 50% of the workforce in 1980 to less than 30% today.[29] The phenomenon itself has been analysed on several occasions and is usually attributed to the shift from an industry based to a services based economy (industrial activity being relocated to low wage countries), combined with increased individualism and desire for diversification in setting terms and conditions of employment.

This trend is not likely to remain without consequences as the Finnish rapporteur indicated, on the basis of many years of experience. It takes little to start an industrial dispute, but it takes a strong union to end such a dispute. It is therefore to the detriment of all parties concerned if union membership is dropping so dramatically.

It was also noted that trade union affiliation on the one hand, and coverage by collective agreements on the other, are two different issues. In the Netherlands, for example, roughly 28% trade union affiliation stands next to more than 80% coverage by collective agreements. Yet, trade unions always had an important role to play in monitoring employer compliance with collective agreements, as well as with legislation. It seems the system may be in need of re-balancing.

A special case is constituted by Eastern Europe, where, after the recent transition to the market economy, there is as yet hardly any practice of social partners bargaining and working together. In many of these countries, trade union affiliation is extremely low, often less than 10%.

7 Decentralization and Europeanization

The logical next step (and theme) is whether works councils could take over the role of trade unions – also in view of the plant/enterprise centred tendency in bargaining. Next to decentralization stand supra-nationalization and its consequences for dispute handling: the gradual development of European bargaining.[30]

---

[29] For a comparative overview see R. Blanpain (ed.), 'Worker's Participation', special issue of the *Bulletin of Comparative Labour Relations*, Kluwer: Deventer 1992. Also see the website http://www.eiro.eurofound.ie/2004/07feature/eu0407207f.

[30] Mundella (in Britain), Vavoissier (in France) and Van Marken (in the Netherlands) are well-known names associated with 19th century initiatives that were essentially local in origin, see A. de Roo and R. Jagtenberg, *Settling Labour Disputes in Europe*, o.c.

There was widespread recognition of the fact that national works councils traditions differ, and that the concept of the European works council (EWC) constitutes yet another model.[31] In the German system, the trade unions managed to attain a foothold in many a council and thus turn these into a mere extension of union bargaining power. According to the German rapporteur, works councils only function well if these are backed by the support of the unions. In the model prevailing in Belgium (and *e.g.* in Italy) the unions have an acknowledged part to play in the council election procedure. The EWC is obviously not based on the German or the Belgian model, but is necessarily restricted in scope, not only in regard of community-wide undertaking, but also in regard of the mere emphasis on consultation and information. Yet, in the United Kingdom, the works council is perceived as an instrument to undermine the unions.

With such diametrically opposed perceptions, it does not seem likely that works councils can take over the role of unions. Apart from that, other fundamental differences remain. Thus, as the German rapporteur pointed out, works councils, in the process of negotiating agreements, may not resort to strikes. This is still a monopoly of the unions bargaining a classical collective agreement.

The Belgian rapporteur drew attention to the interesting example of Poland, where classical bargaining rights were actually granted to works councils. As the employer indirectly controlled these councils, however, this assignment of bargaining rights was held to be in violation of the ILO conventions.

Parallel to the decrease in coverage of collective agreements stands, paradoxically perhaps, the gradual development of agreements with European coverage. And, more important even is the rise of collective disputes with obvious cross-border dimensions, such as the actions at Renault in Vilvoorde.

There was a shared feeling that the number of such cross-border disputes is bound to increase in number, whereas both unions and employers lack skills and experience to handle such disputes.

A further question would then be whether a European mediation agency could be of assistance to the social partners in the various member states, in a way comparable to the supportive role national mediation agencies played in the development of national social dialogue in the early 20th century, when party-negotiators gradually abandoned their local regional bedrock.[32] Such an increase in scale seems to repeat itself today, albeit with the complication of different cultures and languages being involved.

The German rapporteur pointed out that, although there is a distinct rationale for going this way, national social partners – not only in his country but probably also elsewhere in Europe – would likely demonstrate great reluctance to

31 www.eiro.eurofoun.ie/2004/11/inbrief/pl0411102n.html.

32 Mundella (in Britain), Vavoissier (in France) and Van Marken (in the Netherlands) are well-known names associated with 19th century initiatives that were essentially local in origin, see A. de Roo and R. Jagtenberg, *Settling Labour Disputes in Europe*, o.c.

create an official body that could be perceived as taking over power from existing national agencies.

The Belgian rapporteur drew attention to an even more fundamental problem: within the European Commission itself, there are high ranked officials – notably within the Directorate General responsible for Competition – who are inclined to characterize collective labour agreements as tying clauses, violating European competition rules.

In the Expert Meeting, the view prevailed that a common European approach towards labour standards is needed, whereby regulations would probably be more effective than directives. But at the same time, there was scepticism as to the likelihood of consensus ever to arrive. It was thought more likely that, on the contrary, the era of hard law in labour relations is passed and gone. This would also have its repercussions for the opportunities to mediate disputes on a European scale. An example mentioned was Directive 2002/14 EC establishing a general framework for informing and consulting employees in the European Community. A proposal to grant the works council power to delay closure of the plant concerned, and to use the time extension thus gained for consultation and possibly mediation, was defeated, due to fierce resistance from management.[33]

To this we like to add that two fairly recent documents, *i.e.* the outcome of the 11th United Nations Conference on Trade and Development (UNCTAD XI) and the Report of the (ILO appointed) Global Commission on the Social Dimension of Globalization equally suggest a pessimistic prospect in terms of the promotion of labour rights as human rights on an international scale.[34]

8 (Dis-)incentives to negotiation

The abovementioned discussion on hard and soft law leads us into the next theme: the pressure (ensuing from global competition) towards a partnership approach, and the related issue of (dis-)incentives to negotiation in a partnership context.

It may be helpful to quote William Brown one more time: "[...] the emerging picture is clear. The opening up of the world economy and of the public services to wider competition is changing the nature of third party intervention. There is diminishing scope for employers and trade unions to battle out their differences in the sheltered arena of a national market or monopoly service. To do so is to risk annihilation. Trade unions are being forced to shift their manner of operating away from confrontation, towards much greater reliance on co-operation with employers. [...] The implications for third party agencies are far-reaching. [...] The question to be resolved becomes not what is implied by law, but what will work because it is locally felt to reflect reality."[35]

33 www.eiro.eurofoun.ie/2004/11/inbrief/pl0411102n.html.

34 Philip Alston, *Labour Rights as Human Rights*, Oxford University Press: Oxford 2005, 5.

35 Brown, *o.c.*, 8.

This trend first became apparent in traditionally open, export-oriented economies, such as the Netherlands, but is now proliferating throughout Europe. The British rapporteur confirmed the impact on bargaining strategies. In his experience, in the private sector particularly, parties have to weigh up the pros and cons of old distributive bargaining against modern integrative bargaining models. Win-win models are gaining more popularity. Will the identification of common interests become the primary focus in future mediations? But before discussing the possibly changing role of mediators (this will be the subject of theme 8), the preliminary question to be answered is: what will be the characteristics of negotiations in the new partnership model? To put it a bit more bluntly: is there anything left to negotiate at all?

The Chair asked the rapporteurs to consider which factors, in their view, are to be regarded as incentives or disincentives respectively for (still) negotiating successfully.

The German rapporteur contended that, in his opinion, there are three factors conducive to successful bargaining. First, the actors on both sides of the classical collective negotiation table must be strong and reliable. Where union affiliation is low, strike rates tend to be high.

Second, at plant level, the fostering of a process of continuous dialogue may also greatly contribute to harmonious relations, to the coming about of agreements, and to prevention of escalation.

Third, effective conflict resolution schemes are also conducive to constructive relationships. For individual disputes over rights, such effective conflict resolution should be offered by the courts. For collective disputes over interests, conciliation and mediation are the preferred methods of dispute resolution.

General support was expressed for this three-tier observation.

Conversely, what are the potential hurdles to negotiation? Apart from a clair obscur of the preceding observations (so, for instance, weak unions constituting a hurdle), the following aspects were brought up for discussion: situations where (near-) agreements turn out to be unacceptable to some constituencies, or – even more fundamental – irreconcilable with the public interest.

The problem of acceptability to some (or many) but not to all, is highly relevant, in view of the on-going decrease of coverage of agreements and desire for diversification in setting terms and conditions of employment, a development that is equally tied to the globalization process.

The remedy of partial acceptability is found to lie in opening clauses. A shared experience is that in industry-wide agreements over the last 10 years, parties frequently agree to inserting opening clauses, initially for issues such as working time, but recently also on the hard core subject of salary levels, so as to be able to respond to emerging variable needs.[36]

[36] The Belgian rapporteur warned that recommendations such as the one issued by the OECD, that employers should be able to insert opening up facilities one-sidedly, will not be conducive to retaining constructive bargaining systems.

What if (imminent) agreements are found to be in breach of the general interest? This situation likely arises where an agreement contravenes set economic policy targets or wage levels. Sweden constitutes an interesting country in this respect. As the Swedish rapporteur indicated, in such situations a mediator obviously cannot prevent the employer and the union from reaching the agreement. But neither would it fall within the task of the mediator to promote efficient wage formation, if he would stimulate such agreements, particularly as one such agreement creates the risk of knock-on effects, spiralling wage levels, inflation and the like.

The Netherlands also constitutes an interesting case in view of its historical exceptionally interventionist wage policy. According to the Dutch employer's representative, the government has genuinely shifted the responsibility for the outcome of negotiations to the social partners, following the 1982 Wassenaar agreement. The Ministry of Social Affairs will only check compatibility of collective agreements with formal law, not with economic policy. Although at times the Minister threatened to deny general applicability in law to collective agreements for that very reason, the Minister also retracted, in the awareness that one cannot take one brick out of the wall without fundamentally damaging the whole system.

9 A changing role for mediation

This takes us to the next theme. Does all this amount to a changing role for mediation, and mediators? Is there any need left at all for modern mediation techniques?

The answer to this question was decisively positive.

The British rapporteur observed a clear trend away from formal conciliation, whereby the mediator is only involved once a deadlock has occurred towards rendering assistance in negotiations. This development implies that Acas is called in to assist now during earlier stages, before a formal failure to agree arises. Although the old policy, to intervene only in case of a deadlock, may be reflecting party autonomy in the most absolute way, parties may already have become entrenched in their positions. The British experience shows that industrial action by itself hardly ever had the outcomes desired. Mediators experienced in managing change, rather than handling disputes, may be better for the purpose of overall efficacy.

Turning to literature, Brown strikingly concludes that, "[...] accompanying the shift to voluntary dispute resolution, the most important development has been the growth of an advisory function for third party agencies. This advisory role reflects a wider change in conception, evident for many public services, that prevention is better than treatment."[37]

[37] Brown, *o.c.* 6.

A trend thus seems to become manifest, whereby mediation is increasingly regarded as a tool of – what has become known as – 'conflict management'.

In conflict management, relationships are analysed in context, and a variety of well-researched intervention techniques is being deployed in close consultation with the parties, and depending on the specific subject matter at stake. The long-term objective is that parties adopt a more rational and comprehensive approach towards handling conflicts and no longer let themselves be taken by surprise whenever a conflict crops up.[38]

All this implies that the corpus of modern mediation and conflict management techniques is only likely to assume greater significance.

Hence, it seems there is a future for mediation. If the diagnosis of the Expert Meeting is correct, then the social partners may now increasingly be in need of assistance by skilled mediators. Social partners have problems to come to grips with new developments such as globalization, outsourcing and new technologies. The pace of change is high and both sides tend to be conservative in their thinking. Here lies the real problem. Both employers and unions increasingly seem to lack necessary negotiation skills. Perhaps under the pressure of developments as abovementioned, skills hitherto presented are gradually lost. At the same time, negotiations are proliferating to many more fora – notably local fora – where negotiation skills may never have been a key asset anyway.

This is not to say that mediation will have more than a subsidiary role to play. Naturally, parties take pride in succeeding in their direct negotiations and may see it as a failure to resort to mediation. But they do fail from time to time. The added value of mediation will always remain that it can be curative, helping the parties finding a way out of the deadlock. Next there is the development towards conflict management, where the potential of mediation to trace the causes of future problems may be exploited to the full.

But will there still be a need then for state supported third party agencies, as providers of such knowledge and expertise?

Reverting to Brown once again: "Are they (the state supported third party agencies) not another candidate for privatization? Cannot employment relations, like any other business transaction, be facilitated by commercial brokers?"[39]

The answer to this question, however, should be: no. Brown continues: "[...] however much the outcome (of third party assisted collective bargaining) may be constrained by harsh competitive necessity, it is unavoidably bound up with notions of fairness and of natural – if not legal – justice. Settlements that are perceived to be 'unfair' undermine employee morale and sour the employment relationship. [...] third party roles only carry credibility when those who hold them are clearly independent. They have to be seen to be independent of employers, and of trade unions, but also of governments, which often have their own agendas."

---

38 H. Falconer, *Managing Conflict in the Workplace*, LexisNexis: London, 2004.

39 Brown, *o.c.*, 8.

10 Where do we go from here?

The final theme emerged towards the end of the Expert Meeting: is there a value inherent in experienced mediators and academic scholars from the various European countries meeting together as we did on the 3rd of June?

In other words: do the participants constitute a valuable network, to be fostered in the years to come?

The answer was decisively yes. But it should be a network with modest aims, such as exchanging information and deepening our knowledge of what exists. On that basis, common definitions could be worked out in the future. Likewise, issues such as the quality of mediation and conflict management processes could be addressed, from a comparative approach. The combination of practitioners and academics was found to be very helpful, and conducive to considerable cross-pollination. The number of participants should preferably be extended in the future to other countries to do justice to all industrial relations traditions in Europe, and in order to make comparisons more accurate. It is important to realize however, that we are still a long way from acting as an international (European) fire brigade that can operate on call. But then again, every long journey starts with a tiny first step.

CHAPTER 3

Labour dispute resolution and settlement in EU perspective

Frank Hendrickx

Most likely, the best way to deal with labour disputes is to avoid them. The opposite of a labour dispute would probably qualify as industrial peace or, on an individual employer-employee level, as mutual trust and confidence. It would appear that the European Union has been active in promoting such peace rather than providing for specific tools in the area of dispute settlement and resolution. This may not merely result from weakness of action or even a lack of competence, but might also be envisaged as a strong and ambitious concept of labour dispute resolution and settlement.

Nevertheless, if one looks at the EU context of labour dispute resolution issues, it is important to deal with the concepts first. Taking the whole area and development of modern labour law, the EU integration process is far from being fully completed and at its end. Therefore, labour dispute resolution ideas have to be explained from their respective national backgrounds and in a comparative perspective. In this comparative respect, it can be pointed out that the terms 'conflict' or 'dispute' resolution are often used in various places, but not in a uniform manner.[1] In certain systems, 'conflict' embraces both difference of opinion as well as situations in which there is a recognized difference and in which parties stop talking and resort to industrial action. Also the difference between an individual and collective dispute can be made according to the party that raised the issue, but also following the nature of the interest involved. Here, too, a further distinction can be made between disputes over rights and disputes over interests. In a more time-related perspective, dispute resolution can be related to dispute prevention. It seems appropriate here to use the broad definition given by De Roo and Jagtenberg of 'labour disputes' as 'all disputes arising from the conclusion, existence or termination of individual employment contracts and/or collective labour agreements'.[2]

In this chapter, the EU perspectives on labour dispute resolution will be examined. This will be done by providing insight into industrial relations law in the EU, on the assumption that collective labour relations have to be concentrated upon before exploring ideas on dispute resolution or settlement policies or practices. Industrial relations will be discussed not only in terms of collective bargaining, but also within the context of information, consultation and other involvement procedures and practices provided within the context of EU labour law, like those that have been established by regulations on European works councils or the role of worker involvement in the *'Societas Europea'*. It is, however, not the purpose of this contribution to give a detailed and complete description of all worker involvement measures. Rather, assessed elements will be provided in a more synthetic way to put European collective labour law – or industrial relations law – in (future) perspectives of labour dispute resolution in the EU.

---

1 T. Hanami and R. Blanpain, Introductory Remarks and a Comparative Overview, in: *Industrial Conflict Resolution in Market Economies*, T. Hanami and R. Blanpain (eds.), Kluwer: Deventer 1984, 7.

2 A. de Roo and R. Jagtenberg, *Settling Labour Disputes in Europe*, Doctoral thesis, Kluwer Law International: Deventer/Boston 1994, 11.

1 Introductory remarks on EU approaches with regard to labour dispute resolution

As this contribution explores EU perspectives with regard to labour dispute resolution and settlement, it is necessary to indicate the focus of EU law in this area, according to the various dispute resolution channels or strategies.

1.1 Labour dispute resolution channels in the EU

In labour law, different channels may be indicated with regard to either labour law enforcement or labour dispute resolution. In a schematic manner, three of those channels can be pointed out:[3]

- an industrial relations channel: in which mainly the social partners (workers and employers organizations) are involved and are playing the main role. It encompasses all kinds of institutions, procedures and practices whereby the use of dialogue and negotiations can be seen as tools of problem and dispute solving;
- an administrative channel: an enforcement or resolution process or procedure, involving administrative or arbitration institutions, reporting or other mechanisms, mostly involving state involvement;
- a judicial channel: dispute settlement by tribunals and courts.

It is obvious that the choice for either one of the channels is dependent on many variables, but also to the extent that disputes over rights or disputes over interests are concerned.

At the EU level, the judicial channel as such is well developed. But some important qualifications have to be made. Dependent on competence, labour law enforcement issues can be brought before the European Court of Justice, which has a strongly developed case law in this area. It is less evident, due to the nature and the context of European Community law, to see labour disputes (with no state actor involved) being solved.

The administrative channel has not been very much developed at EU level. There is, for example, no real administrative remedy in the area of labour law, nor is there a European labour arbitration institution.

The highest attention at the EU level has been focused on the channel of industrial relations. Although it is still incomplete, industrial relations have been recognized in EC Treaty mechanisms, and information and consultation have been on the forefront in various EU measures.

---

3 See categories used in J. Malmberg, *Effective Enforcement of EC Labour Law*, Kluwer Law International: The Hague, 59 (although we prefer a slightly adapted version).

1.2 Policy strategies

It has been suggested that one view of looking at worker participation is to see it as an important means for the resolution of industrial conflicts.[4] This brings us to the policy strategies with regard to labour dispute resolution. There are different devices to prevent open conflict or to limit it as far as possible and to arrive at overall acceptable solutions. These include positive and negative policy interventions:[5]

The negative policy interventions are: prohibition of industrial action in certain areas of activity, such as the army, police or other public sector services; the provision of essential services in the private sector; unilateral governmental decision-making; the peace obligation; cooling off periods; obligatory mediation, conciliation or fact-finding.

The positive policy interventions are: involving employees in the decision-making process or conflict resolution through information, consultation, collective bargaining, board representation, etc.

It is clear that the EU strongly focuses on the area of industrial relations. But it should be pointed out that the current EC framework is far from imposing a single or uniform industrial relations model. As Schregle has pointed out, "[...] in every country, North and South, workers, employers and governments have both common and divergent interests, short term and long term. The divergent interests should be accommodated and reconciled. The way in which such interests are expressed and reconciled is the subject of industrial relations. This will necessarily vary from country to country."[6] Although such necessity in these variations may be discussed or questioned, it still lies underneath EC labour law. The issue of 'industrial relations' regulation in the EU is examined below.

1.3 Connecting to the ILO approach

Looking at the ILO's approach, it is striking that dispute prevention and resolution are used under the same rubric: "The dispute prevention and resolution process seeks to assist parties in the employment relationship to settle their grievances or disputes peacefully and orderly through agreed machinery with minimum disruption of work. In a sense, it is a peace-making arrangement. It assumes that disagreement will from time to time occur, where there are different perceptions of what is fair or equitable. At the same time, disputes can be managed, indeed prevented. As such, the effective prevention

4 M. Weiss, S. Simitis and W. Rydzy, The Settlement of Labour Disputes in the Federal Republic of Germany, in: *Industrial Conflict Resolution in Market Economies*, T. Hanami and R. Blanpain (eds.), Kluwer: Deventer 1984, 87-88.

5 T. Hanami and R. Blanpain, Introductory Remarks and a Comparative Overview, in: *Industrial Conflict Resolution in Market Economies*, T. Hanami and R. Blanpain (eds.), Kluwer: Deventer 1984, 2-3.

6 J. Schregle, Comparative Industrial Relations, in: *International Labour Review* 1981, 27.

and settlement of labour disputes remains at the core of sound labour relations and in creating a conducive environment for efficiency, economic growth and development."[7]

Also in the ILO's view, the effective resolution of labour disputes is closely linked to promotion of the right to collective bargaining. In this context the structure of dispute settlement systems is normally designed to promote collective bargaining, for example, by requiring the parties to exhaust all the possibilities of reaching a negotiated solution or to exhaust the dispute settlement procedures provided for by their collective agreement before having access to state provided procedures.[8] According to Convention No. 154, bodies and procedures for the settlement of labour disputes should be so conceived as to contribute to the promotion of collective bargaining (Convention No. 154, Article 5, paragraph 2(e)).

This could imply the existence of a strong parallel between the broader ILO view on labour dispute resolution and the EU's attempts to work towards a system of industrial relations, laying down the basis for dispute resolution channels.

2 The issue of industrial relations law in the EU

Given that the collective aspect is of significant importance in the area of labour dispute resolution or settlement, it is necessary to deal with industrial relations law in the EU.

'Until now the European Union has abstained from regulating on collective bargaining', is a comment often heard.[9] It makes industrial relations law, or collective labour law, quite problematic in the EU. In fact, it marks the nature of EU labour law and social policy as it stands in its current shape.

Indeed, in understanding European social policy, the broader context of European integration should be mentioned. The Union structure as it presently stands and as established by the EU Treaty can only be seen as a provisional structure.[10] Evidence of this is the current debated EU Constitution Treaty. It is made clear by the EU Treaty itself, which states that the Union in its present form is 'a new stage in the process of creating an ever closer union among the peoples of Europe'.[11] We may call this process European integration.[12] It implies

7 www.ilo.org/public/english/dialogue.

8 www.ilo.org/public/english/dialogue.

9 H. Knudsen, Representation and Participation – Unilateralism or Bipartism?, in: *Labour and Employment Regulation in Europe*, J. Lind, H. Knudsen and H. Jorgensen (eds.), Work & Society No. 45, 2004, 27.

10 P.J.G. Kapteyn and P. Verloren van Themaat, *Introduction to the Law of the European Communities. From Maastricht to Amsterdam*, Kluwer Law International: The Hague 1998, 54.

11 Article A, para 2 TEU. (CR).

12 Although it is not clear what the ultimate and future result will be.

that policies, such as social policy, must be seen in their dynamic character. In the present situation – *i.e.* the European Union hosts the European Communities and the supplementary policies and forms of co-operation of the Member States (in three pillars) – social policy, including labour law, belongs mainly to the European Communities (first pillar), which may be considered to constitute the strongest structure of the European Union.

With due regard to the above qualification, the process of European integration could be seen through a concept of 'state forming' or even federalism. But the EU remains a unique structure and conceptualizing the EU through familiar state categories may merely seem a 'classical way of removing the mist' regarding its nature.[13] A useful perspective is to regard the European Union as a form of 'multitiered governance'. In an intergovernmental view of the Union, the central fact is the autonomy of the Member States, which remain sovereign nation-states.[14] In a multitiered governance viewpoint (also indicated as a 'multilevel constitutional system'),[15] decision-making is shared by multiple tiers. It indicates that the transfer of Member State authority to the Union level becomes increasingly embedded in a complex institutional environment 'that cannot easily be described in terms of interstate bargaining'.[16] Yet, it may be argued that the typification of governance of the EU may depend on the context of the consulted literature or the context of the European policy, which is understood.[17] As far as EU social policy is concerned, the European level may clearly be distinguished from the national level. 'What is emerging in Europe is a system of shared political authority over social policy, though one that is far more decentralized than the arrangements of traditional federal states'.[18] Indeed, what distinguishes the European Union from traditional federal systems is the predominant position of the Member States.[19] It may further be argued that the European Union has potentially no competences like those which States possess since it is based on the principle of limited special authorization.[20] By the founding Treaties, the Member States have transferred sovereign powers in

13 J.H.H. Weiler, European Models: Polity, People and System, in: *Lawmaking in the European Union*, P. Craig and C. Harlow (eds.), Kluwer Law International: The Hague 1998, 9.

14 P. Pierson and S. Leibfried, Multitiered Institutions and the Making Of Social policy, in: S. Leibfried and P. Pierson (eds.), *European Social Policy. Between Fragmentation and Integration*, The Brookings Institution: Washington D.C. 1995, 7.

15 J. Shaw, Law of the European Union, in: *Palgrave Law Masters*, Palgrave: Houdmills 2000, 190.

16 P. Pierson and S. Leibfried, *o.c.*, 1995, 6.

17 Cf. J.H.H. Weiler, European Models: Polity, People and System, in: *Lawmaking in the European Union*, P. Craig and C. Harlow (eds.), Kluwer Law International: The Hague 1998, 10-11.

18 P. Pierson and S. Leibfried, *o.c.*, 1995, 4.

19 P. Pierson and S. Leibfried, *o.c.*, 1995, 7.

20 U. Everling, Comments on the article by B. de Witte, in: *Reforming the Treaty on European Union. The Legal Debate*, J.A. Winter, D.M. Curtin, A.E. Kellerman, B. de Witte (eds.), Kluwer Law International: The Hague 1996, 19.

special fields to the Community.[21] In the field of social policy, it concerns shared competences. Neither the Member States, nor the European Community, are exclusively competent for social policy.

2.1 The nature of labour law competences in the EC Treaty

An issue, which has to be referred to, is the extent to which 'industrial relations' law has been developed under the EC 'acquis'. For a good understanding, it is necessary to focus on the 'social chapter' of the EC Treaty first.

The EC Treaty, in order for the Community to realize the high social objectives laid down in Article 136, provides a number of competences, for the EU itself as well as for the social partners. The underlying philosophy is laid down in Article 136 EC Treaty itself:

> "The Community and the Member States, having in mind fundamental social rights such as those set out in the European Social Charter signed at Turin on 18 October 1961 and in the 1989 Community Charter of the Fundamental Social Rights of Workers, shall have as their objectives the promotion of employment, improved living and working conditions, so as to make possible the harmonization while the improvement is being maintained, proper social protection, dialogue between management and labour, the development of human resources with a view to lasting employment and the combating of exclusion. To this end the Community and the Member States shall implement measures which take account of the diverse forms of national practices, in particular in the field of contractual relations, and the need to maintain the competitiveness of the Community economy. They believe that such a development will ensue not only from the functioning of the common market, which will favour harmonization of social systems, but also from the procedures provided for in this Treaty and from the approximation of provisions laid down by law, regulation or administrative action."

In the field of labour law, different forms of community involvement may be distinguished. These vary from co-operation and co-ordination to true legislative competences.

2.2 Legislative competences in the social chapter

Article 137 of the first chapter of Title XI of the EC Treaty allows the Community to formulate regulations, directives or recommendations with either qualified majority or unanimity with a view of achieving the objectives of Article 136 in quite a number of fields, with the exclusion however of 'pay, the right of association, the right to strike or the right to impose lock-outs.' The

[21] U. Everling, *o.c.*, 1996, 19.

'provisions adopted pursuant to this article shall not prevent any Member State from maintaining or introducing more (stringent) protective measures compatible with the Treaty'.[22]

Qualified majority voting

Article 137(1) provides that the Community shall, with a view to achieving the objectives of Article 136, support and complement Member States' activities in a number of fields in which (legislative) intervention with qualified majority is possible:

- improvement in particular of the working environment to protect workers' health and safety;
- working conditions;
- the information and consultation of workers;
- the integration of persons excluded from the labour market;
- equality between men and women with regard to labour market opportunities and treatment at work.

The wording from Article 137 is quite clear. Community intervention in the mentioned areas is restricted to supporting and complementing Member States' activities, and not aimed at replacing them. The EC Treaty further mentions the forms that Community action in the above fields may receive. It stipulates that the Council may adopt, by means of directives, minimum requirements for gradual implementation having regard to the conditions and technical rules obtaining in each of the Member States.[23] It is also stated that the Council, acting in accordance with the same procedure, may adopt measures designed to encourage co-operation between Member States through initiatives aimed at improving knowledge, developing exchanges of information and best practices, promoting innovative approaches and evaluating experiences in order to combat social exclusion.

Unanimous voting

The Council shall act unanimously on a proposal from the Commission, after consulting the European Parliament, the Economic and Social Committee and the Committee of the Regions in the following areas:

- social security and social protection of workers;
- protection of workers where their employment contract is terminated;
- representation and collective defence of the interests of workers and employers, including co-determination;
- conditions of employment for third-country nationals legally residing in Community territory;
- financial contributions for promotion of employment and job-creation, without prejudice to the provisions relating to the Social Fund.

---

22 Article 137(5) EC Treaty.

23 Article 137(2) EC Treaty.

Excluded areas

The provisions of Article 137 do not apply to pay, the right of association, the right to strike or the right to impose lockouts. In other words, these matters are excluded. However, this does not necessarily mean that those fields in no circumstances can be subject to Community action. Still, Community action in these areas will need to be justified on the basis of another Treaty provision.

2.3 Identifying industrial relations at EU level

With a view to the fact that Article 137 of the EC Treaty excludes the right of association and the right to strike from its 'social chapter', one could come to the conclusion that the 'core' rights in industrial relations fall outside the sphere of EU law, although the Charter on Fundamental Rights of the Union (Nice, 2000) may re-introduce these fundamental rights into the EU sphere, but in a rather weak form (*i.e.* not in a legal basis for legislative action).

Nevertheless, some form of industrial relations practices has existed for quite some time at European level.

Social dialogue – and industrial relations – at the European level originated with a series of talks, initiated in the 1980's under the driving force of Commission President Jacques Delors. These discussion rounds concerned informal meetings held at Val Duchesse and were soon labelled as 'social dialogue'. The parties invited to participate in these talks were from the employers' side, Union of Industrial Employers' Confederations of Europe (UNICE) and *Centre Européen des Entreprises Publiques* (*CEEP*), and from the trade union side, European Trade Union Conference (ETUC). Later on, this cross-industry social dialogue was formalized and received a prominent role in the mechanisms of the EC Treaty.

Presently, various social partners can be identified on the European level. The general cross-industry social partners[24] are from the employers' side, UNICE and *CEEP*, and, from the trade union side, ETUC. There are also cross-industry organizations which represent certain categories of workers or undertakings, such as European Association of Craft and Small and Medium-Sized Enterprises (UEAPME), *Eurocadres and Confédération Européenne des Cadres* (*CEC*). Furthermore, there are many industry-level (sector) social partners.[25]

Although it is possible to identify social partners at the European level, there still remain problems. The role of the social partners has been dramatically enhanced on the occasion of the Treaties of Maastricht and Amsterdam (from consultation with the European Community regarding the implementa-

[24] Cf. List of European social-partner organizations consulted under Article 138 of the Treaty, Annex 1 of Communication from the Commission, *The European Social Dialogue, a Force for Innovation and Change*, COM(2002) 34 final of 26 June 2002, 32p.

[25] *E.g.* European Banking Federation (FBE), International Confederation of Temporary Work Business (CIETT-Europe), European Transport Workers' Federation(ETF), European Metalworkers' Federation (EMF).

tion of Community directives to collective bargaining at the European level). In consequence, the social partners are entitled to real involvement in the shaping of European labour law from the initial stages, as well as, for certain countries where this is legally possible, in the implementation of Council directives. At the same time, a stronger legal basis has been laid for European-wide collective bargaining and mechanisms were introduced ensuring a binding effect of European collective agreements *erga omnes*.

Nonetheless, especially regarding these agreements, quite a number of extremely complex problems of a legal nature arise, for the solution of which ultimately further Community legislation may be needed. Within this problematic EU setting, the development of the right to strike, the regulation of collective bargaining and the issue of representation can be mentioned.

Social dialogue and collective bargaining can take place at various levels: at the cross-industry level, at the sector level and at the enterprise level. It can be noted that while social dialogue is recognized in the EC Treaty and by the Commission and identified as a key element of European social policy, there is little European regulation of the subject. In this context, some remarks can be made with regard to the different levels of social dialogue.

Cross-industry level

Since the Val Duchesse dialogue meetings, some form of cross-industry level social dialogue has existed on the European level. With the Amsterdam Treaty, cross-industry level social dialogue has been institutionalized in the Social Chapter of the EC Treaty (inclusion of the Maastricht Agreement on Social Policy). Under Article 138 of the EC Treaty, there is a procedure of obligatory two-stage consultation of the social partners by the Commission (see below).

In addition to the obligatory consultation procedure, the Commission systematically consults the cross-industry social partners on all-important developments in the economic and the social policy fields. Many forms of consultation on Community policies take place in the advisory committees, set up by the Commission since the 1960's. These are tripartite fora whose role is to advise the Commission on the formulation of specific policies and assist it in their implementation.

Sector level

Social dialogue at sector level has existed on the European level for a long time. Since the 1960's, the Commission set up various sectoral committees, either under the form of Joint Committees or as informal working groups. The sector-specific consultations are aimed at improving and harmonizing working conditions and also, in some cases, improving the economic and competitive position of the sector concerned.[26] In an effort to achieve a more harmonized

[26] COM(98)322 of 20 May 1998, p. 7.

and effective approach to the structures of sector dialogue, the Commission adopted a Decision on 20 May 1998, providing a framework for Sectoral Dialogue Committees.

According to the Decision of 20 May 1998, Sectoral Dialogue Committees are established in those sectors where the social partners make a joint request to take part in a dialogue at the European level, and where the organizations representing both sides of industry fulfil the following criteria:

1) relate to specific sectors or categories and be organized at the European level;
2) consist of organizations which are themselves an integral and recognized part of Member States' social partner structures and with the capacity to negotiate agreements, and which are representative of several Member States;
3) have adequate structures to ensure their effective participation in the work of the Committees.

On this basis, the Commission has been able to create about 27 committees at the joint request of the social partners in various sectors. The committees have given rise to some 230 commitments of different types, such as opinions, common positions, declarations, guidelines, codes of conduct, charters and agreements.[27]

Enterprise level

According to the European Commission, "European integration encourages companies to develop on a transnational scale. Reinforcing European or transnational dialogue among firms has become a fundamental challenge for tomorrow's Europe, particularly in regard to mobility, pensions and equivalence of qualifications."[28] Enterprise social dialogue and bargaining on the European level can be identified through European group works councils established in more than 700 transnational undertakings in Europe following the adoption of Directive 94/45/EC on European works councils, although works councils have not been traditionally envisaged for bargaining but for representation purposes.

3 Industrial relations through social dialogue under the EC Treaty

In order to understand the actual operation of EU industrial relations, the role of social dialogue under the EC Treaty has to be envisaged. We

[27] Numbers of 2002, cf. *The Sectoral Dialogue in Europe*, European Commission, Employment & Social Affairs, Office for Official Publications of the European Communities, Luxembourg 2003, 10.

[28] COM(2002)341 final of 26 June 2002, 11.

limit ourselves to the role in Community law making, either through consultation, or through European collective bargaining.

3.1 The role of social partners in the legislative process under the social chapter

The social partners can play various roles in the making of European law, which take the form of consultation, intervention and initiative. However, not necessarily are results of social dialogue or collective bargaining legally binding in their nature.

Consultation

While, in principle, the Commission has the power to initiate the legislative process under the EC Treaty, in making a proposal of legislation to the Council, the EC Treaty has provided for a specific role of the social partners in this process.

Under Article 138 of the EC Treaty, there is a procedure of obligatory consultation of the social partners by the Commission. This consultation consists of two stages.

1. First stage consultation: Article 138, 2 of the EC Treaty provides that, before submitting proposals in the social policy field, the Commission shall consult management and labour on the possible direction of Community action;
2. Second stage consultation: According to Article 138, 3 of the EC Treaty, if, after such (first stage) consultation, the Commission considers Community action advisable, it shall consult management and labour on the content of the envisaged proposal. Management and labour shall forward to the Commission an opinion or, where appropriate, a recommendation.

According to the Commission,[29] the two-stage consultation has a dual purpose:

- the opinions of the interested parties can be taken into account and the impact of any legislation assessed. The Commission can thus formulate policies appropriate, in their form and substance, to the problems dealt with and incorporate the aim of social modernization and improving companies' competitiveness;
- the outcome may be independent social dialogue, multi-sectoral or sectoral, and ultimately, therefore, agreements which may subsequently be incorporated into Community law. This is a practical application of the principle of social subsidiarity. It is for the social players to make the first move to arrive at appropriate solutions coming within their area of responsibility; the Community institutions intervene, at the Commission's initiative, only where negotiations fail.

---

[29] COM(2002)341 final of 26 June 2002.

This compulsory consultation under Article 138 of the EC Treaty is additional to the consultations that take place within the context of advisory committees, which operate under the supervision of the European Commission.

Intervention

Article 138, section 4 of the EC Treaty provides that, on the occasion of such consultation, management and labour may inform the Commission of their wish to initiate the process provided for in Article 139. The duration of the procedure shall not exceed nine months, unless the management and labour concerned and the Commission decide jointly to extend it.

This means that the social partners may intervene in the legislative process initiated by the European Commission by informing the latter that they wish to proceed on their own in regulating the subject by concluding a European-wide agreement (as provided under Article 139 of the EC Treaty).

According to Article 138, 4 of the EC Treaty, the duration of the procedure shall not exceed 9 months, unless the management and labour concerned and the Commission decide jointly to extend it.

Initiative

The EC Treaty explicitly provides the possibility for the social partners to conclude a Community-wide agreement at any time and on their own free initiative. Article 139, section 1 of the EC Treaty stipulates that, should management and labour so desire, the dialogue between them at Community level may lead to contractual relations, including agreements. According to Article 139, section 2 of the EC Treaty, these European agreements can be implemented in two main ways:

- either in accordance with the procedures and practices specific to management and labour and the Member States; or
- in matters covered by Article 137, at the joint request of the signatory parties, by a Council decision on a proposal from the Commission.

In the case where social partners would conclude a Community-wide agreement, either on the inter-industry level, or on the level of a given sector, the ultimate legal character of the instrument is partly dependent upon the will of the parties themselves. They can decide to conclude a binding agreement, but they also keep the freedom to structure the result of their bargaining in a common opinion, a recommendation or a code of practice. In the following paragraph, the European collective bargaining agreement will be discussed more closely.

3.2 European collective agreement

As explained above, employers' organizations and employees' organizations can conclude collective agreements on the European level. In labour law, a collective agreement is often defined as an agreement between one or more employers or employers' organizations and one or more employees' organizations, concerning the terms and conditions of employment and the rights and the obligations of the contracting parties.

While Articles 138 and 139 of the EC Treaty have forced a break-through in European labour law and social policy, European Community law does not contain specific provisions with regard to European collective agreements. In the absence of such specific European legal rules, many questions remain as to which legal rules should apply in case a collective agreement is concluded at the European level. In many cases, national law will be applicable to an agreement which is concluded at the European level. There is even scope for parties to determine which law will govern the European collective agreement. As indicated above, social dialogue and collective bargaining may also lead, according to the wish of the parties, to non-binding agreements, such as recommendations or codes of practice.

As explained above, according to Article 139, 2 EC Treaty, a European collective agreement may be implemented in two main ways:

1) Implementation in Accordance with National Practice

This form does not imply any obligation on the Member States to apply the agreements directly or to work out rules for their transposition. Neither is there any obligation to amend national legislation in force to facilitate their implementation. This means that the European agreements will have to be implemented in the Member States through the collective bargaining system itself, which is prevalent at (national) level in each country.

2) Implementation by a Council Decision

The Council can, at the joint request of the signatory parties and on a proposal from the Commission, implement an agreement by a decision. The Council and the Commission can of course only act in matters for which they are competent on the basis of the EC Treaty.

This procedure of implementation, which normally goes through a Council Directive, has already been used for some inter-industry agreements, but also for a number of sectoral collective agreements.

4 Industrial relations through institutionalized procedures and practices

Information and consultation of employees has always been part of the European social agenda, practically since the beginning of the 1960s. However, from the beginning and towards the early 1970s, no specific worker involvement measures can be found. The most important factor herein is probably the fact that any such measure would have to be conceived against the background of disparate systems of industrial relations in European Member States,[30] which made consensus over these subjects obviously difficult. It was

[30] M. Fuchs, The Bottom Line of European Labour Law, in: *I.J.C.L.I.R.* 2004, Vol. 20/3, 437.

economic factors, therefore, that gave rise to (collective) labour law becoming an issue.

4.1 European initiatives in the field of restructuring

During the 1970s, questions arose as to whether or not Europe should intervene in the process of business restructuring and, in particular, set a number of minimum rules to protect the rights of employees in this respect. Doing so would not only improve worker protection, but also facilitate transborder restructuring of the enterprise.

This line of thinking gave birth, basically, to three directives:

- Directive 01/23/EG[31] on transfer of undertakings;
- Directive 75/129/EEG, amended by Directive 98/59/EG on collective redundancies;
- Directive 80/987/EEG,[32] amended by 02/74/EG[33] on insolvency of the employer.

These directives have to be put in their relevant timeframe. The directives are products of the 1970s, in the sense that they reflect the economic realities of that period, with high unemployment and closures of enterprises. All this justified European legal intervention on the basis of Article 100 (current Article 94) of the EC Treaty.

All three instruments mentioned above also reflect a rather modest view on how industrial relations should operate in times of crisis. Looking at the content of the directives, it appears that they do not interfere with the management's rights of decision, but rather involve the workers representatives with a view to regulating and mitigating the social consequences of restructuring.

4.2 European initiatives in the field of worker involvement

Although various views may be defended in this regard, the beginning of the workers' participation issue is often related to the so-called Vredeling proposal, named after the then Social Commissioner H. Vredeling, which was adopted by the Commission on 24 October 1980 concerning the information and consultation of employees employed in undertakings with a complex structure, especially multinational enterprises. The target of the proposal was both the national enterprise and the group as a whole, so that local management would be in a position to give the employees of the subsidiary a clear picture of the activities of the undertaking as a whole, when this undertak-

[31] O.J. 2001, L 82/16.

[32] O.J. 1998, L 225/16.

[33] O.J. 2002, L 270/10.

ing operates in various' countries. Secondly, the proposal intended to provide for the local workers' representatives to have access to top management when information at a local level would be insufficient. Finally its purpose was that local management would be able to provide the workers' representatives with adequate information at a local level and with consultation opportunities regarding important decisions affecting local conditions that would be taken at distant headquarters.

Few proposals have aroused such heated debate as the Vredeling proposal. Both camps entrenched themselves. Everybody proclaimed that employees were entitled to information and consultation. The way in which this had to be organized and the dimension involved were other matters. A consensus between the social partners seemed impossible and in addition the governments were deeply divided. An amended proposal for a directive on procedures for informing and consulting employees of 13 July 1983 was equally unsuccessful and the Vredeling proposal was buried. The problem was postponed and was to be discussed in 1989, but nothing happened and the Vredeling proposal belongs to history. The Commission would nevertheless, within the framework of the social action programme of 1990, prepare an 'instrument concerning the information and consultation of employees.'

This took the form of a proposal for a directive on the establishment of a European Works Council in Community-scale undertakings or groups of undertakings for the purpose of informing and consulting employees and of a directive on information and consultation. At the end, this resulted in three sets of instruments.

In the field of worker involvement, the following instruments have to be mentioned:

- Council Directive 94/45/EC of 22 September 1994 on the establishment of a European Works Council or a procedure in Community-scale undertakings and Community-scale groups of undertakings for the purposes of informing and consulting employees;[34]
- Council Regulation (EC) No. 2157/2001 of 8 October 2001 on the Statute for a European company (SE), and Council Directive 2001/86/EC of 8 October 2001 supplementing the Statute for a European company with regard to the involvement of employees;[35]
- Directive 2002/14/EC of the European Parliament and of the Council of 11 March 2002 establishing a general framework for informing and consulting employees in the European Community.

[34] Including Council Directive 97/74/EC of 15 December 1977 extending, to the United Kingdom of Great Britain and Northern Ireland, Directive 94/45/EC on the establishment of a European Works Council or a procedure in Community-scale undertakings and Community-scale groups of undertakings for the purposes of informing and consulting employees.

[35] Also Council Regulation (EC) No. 1435/2003 of 22 July 2003 on the Statute for a European Cooperative Society (SCE), and Council Directive 2003/72/EC of 22 July 2003 supplementing the Statute for a European Co-operative Society with regard to the involvement of employees.

5 Evaluating EU perspectives on labour dispute resolution

With regard to the three labour dispute channels mentioned above (judicial, administrative, industrial relations), it has been pointed out that the EU has strongly focused on the latter. No particular measure on labour mediation, conciliation or arbitration can be indicated. This does not take away that a European interest exists, as can be shown by the studies undertaken under EU initiation.[36]

Hereafter, an attempt is made to evaluate EU perspectives on labour dispute resolution, by drawing some synthesis of the various industrial relations patterns and strategies that underlie European social policy. It is left up to appreciation whether they may become real building stones for the further prospects in this area, but likely they provide for deeper insight in that regard.

Industrial relations policy approaches

In general, EU social policy may be considered to lay strong emphasis on a preventive approach with regard to labour dispute resolution. In line with the ILO view on labour dispute settlement, European policy is conceived to contribute to the promotion of collective bargaining (cf. ILO Convention No. 154, Article 5, paragraph 2(e)). In fact, it may be argued that EU policy and collective labour law is aimed at laying ground for the (further) development of EU industrial relations. This implies a strong triggering at the third labour dispute resolution channel.

There are two ways of voicing interests collectively in industrial relations: the first is based on trade union membership and collective bargaining, while the second is based on statutory rights to information, consultation and participation in management decisions.[37] Clearly, the EU has worked on both areas.

In the first place, the development of collective bargaining is built in the EC Treaty's social chapter. Under the Treaty, the European Commission has the task to promote social dialogue.

The other route is laid down in the secondary legislation. For example, as one of the resulting consequences from the directive on European works councils (EWC), it is argued that it is not only possible, but also real, that existing EWC processes and practices may lead to the development of trade union networks.[38]

Obviously, this (double) strategy shows intrinsic problems. The basic legal competences, such as those with regard to the right to strike or the right to

[36] Fernando Valdés Dal-Ré, *Synthesis Report on Conciliation, Mediation and Arbitration in the European Union Countries*, March 2002, 25p.

[37] H. Knudsen, Representation and Participation – Unilateralism or Bipartism?, in: *Labour and Employment Regulation in Europe*, Work & Society, No. 49, 2004, 25.

[38] B. Tully, Organising Across Borders. Developing Trade Union Networks, in: *European Works Councils, Pessimism of the Intellect, Optimism of the Will?*, I. Fitzgerald and J. Stirling (eds.), Routledge: London 2004, 165.

freedom of association, have been excluded from the EC Treaty's social chapter. On top of this, it should be mentioned that there is a lack of real transnational industrial relations. Further, there is the lack of uniformity of rules and practices of Member States' industrial relations. In the words of Preamble No. 5, the directive on employee involvement in the *Societas Europea*: "The great diversity of rules and practices existing in the Member States as regards the manner in which employees' representatives are involved in decision-making within companies makes it inadvisable to set up a single European model of employee involvement applicable to the *Societas Europea*."

Still, a preventive approach is also found to be present in the strategies of modern trade unionism. As Hyman as pointed out, one of the challenges of international trade unionism is to have the ability "[...] to develop a proactive agenda rather than simply reacting to management's agenda; the internal democratic life ('internal solidarity'), which enables members to identify with, or in the current jargon to 'own' the policies pursued on their behalf'."[39]

Embryonic (dispute resolution) strategies or tactics

Although there is no real policy in the area of dispute resolution, some embryonic signs of strategies or tactics in this area can be mentioned. It is clear that they mostly concern the industrial relations dispute resolution channel, in which the Commission also takes initiatives at various sector levels, to develop administrative-like practices. Most of them also concern preventive approaches of dispute avoidance, rather than post-conflict resolution.

Interest bargaining

In American literature, the issue of 'interest arbitration' is currently discussed. It is described as a means of avoiding the harmful consequences of strikes and lockouts in a fragile and increasingly interdependent economy. What is proposed is the setting up of a procedure, to which the parties agree, whereby the arbitrator's award will not be final until the parties have had an opportunity during a fairly brief period to see if they can negotiate an agreement that both prefer to the arbitrator's award.[40]

There are some similarities with what exists under the EC Treaty. The mechanisms under the EC Treaty allow tactics, whereby the European Commission may use a directive proposal to force the social partners to reach an agreement, which they would prefer rather than a legislative instrument. This process has been described under the well-known terms of Bercusson's 'bargaining in the shadow of the law' or Blanpain's 'Damocles bargaining.' Translated to the subject of this contribution, one may speak of 'interest bargaining'.

39 R. Hyman, Solidarity for Ever?, in: *Labour and Employment Regulation in Europe*, Work & Society, No. 45, 2004, 44.

40 S.B. Goldberg, A Modest Proposal for Better Integrating Collective Bargaining and Interest Arbitration, *Labor Lawyer* 2003, Vol. 19, 97, 100.

Bargaining in good faith and the SNB

Although no regulation on collective bargaining exists under EC labour law, the current measures show strong parallels with the concept of 'bargaining in good faith'. The concept of negotiating "with a view to reach an agreement" is used in many instances.

Under the Transfer of Undertakings Directive, both the transferor and transferee are required to inform the representatives of their respective employees affected by a transfer of the following (Article 7(1)):

- the date or proposed date of the transfer;
- the reasons for the transfer;
- the legal, economic and social implications of the transfer for the employees;
- any measures envisaged in relation to the employees.

The transferor must provide this information in good time before the transfer is carried out. The transferee must provide it in good time, and in any event before its employees are directly affected by the transfer as regards their conditions of work and employment. Whereas the obligation to provide information is general, the consultation obligation is limited. This obligation exists when the transferor or transferee envisages measures in relation to his employees (Article 7(2)), *e.g.* a reduction in the size of the workforce. Consultation, nevertheless, takes place 'with a view to seeking agreement'. The Court of Justice has interpreted a similar provision in Directive 75/129/EEC (collective redundancies), although as not creating an obligation with regard to results.[41]

A similar idea has been created under the European works council directive, in which Article 6 refers to negotiation between central management and the Special Negotiating Body (SNB) 'in a spirit of co-operation' and 'with a view to reach an agreement'. A comparable obligation is laid down in Article 4 of the *Societas Europea* Worker Involvement Directive. Both directives mentioned here also have found it useful to introduce the SNB. Such SNB has the task of determining with central management the content and scope of agreement that has to be concluded in the directives' respect frameworks, usually composed of worker representatives of various Member States subsidiaries. The fact that this system has been repeated by following directives might provide a (although conditional) belief that an SNB has also potentials in dispute resolution policies.

Virtual bargaining and the role of Ewc

Ewcs may serve as information-oriented platforms of mediation in transnational companies. While not being responsible for uniform European bargaining on levels of pay and working conditions, a form of 'virtual collective bargaining' may take place, whereby union or worker representatives do not negotiate face-to-face at the European level, but in which negotiating positions and bargaining

[41] Case 284/83, *Dansk Metalarbejderforbund*.

outcomes within the different national operations of the enterprise are co-ordinated across countries.[42] In this sense, Ewcs may act as a mediating point[43] for the various national bargaining processes.

It should still be noted that the Ewc dynamics do not always play a significant role in 'crisis management' or problem solving, let alone dispute resolution. As has been shown in the 2000 'BMW-Rover'-case, the Ewc was practically unaware of the selling plans developed by central management.[44] Ewcs still seem to have little impact on management decision-making. Management also seems to be reluctant to consult the Ewc in due time, fearing sensitive information to be released. This obviously hampers the Ewc in playing its possible preventive role in labour dispute resolution strategies.[45]

Cooling off periods

Cooling off periods are typical instruments of dispute resolution in times of conflict between management and employees, typically in the context of corporate restructuring. The concept is also used by the European legislator. Looking at the Collective Redundancies Directive, Article 4 provides that a cooling off period of 30 shall be respected after notification of the workers' representatives of projected collective dismissals. In practice, such period can be used to negotiate on tailored solutions.

Crisis management and sector mediation

Worker participation is often seen as a means in terms of the influence of the workforce in management's decision making.[46] However, the involvement of workers in corporate life may be a powerful tool in the management of crises. This is well seen in the document on 'managing change' and the partnership idea developed by the European Commission on a number of occasions.

In its recent Communication on restructuring and employment, the Commission concentrates it views on a sector approach, whereby the sector dialogue Committees, set up by the Commission in various sectors, may move forward towards sector mediation structures in times of crisis.

---

42 P. Marginson, The Eurocompany and Euro Industrial Relations, in: *European Journal of Industrial Relations*, Vol. (6)1, 2000, 30.

43 Term used in M. Martinez Lucio and S. Weston, European Works Councils. Structures and Strategies in the New Europe, in: *European Works Councils. Pessimism of the intellect, optimism of the will?*, Routledge: London 2004, 40.

44 Ch. Villiers, The Rover Case (A). The Sale of Rover Cars by BMW – the Role of the Works Council, in: *I.L.J.* 2000, 386.

45 P. Lorber, Reviewing the European Works Council Directive: European Progress and United Kingdom Pespective, in: *I.L.J.* 2000, 193.

46 M. Weiss, Workers' Participation in the European Union, in: *European Community Labour Law. Principles and Perspectives, Liber Amicorum Lord Wedderburn*, Clarendon Press: Oxford 1996, 213.

CHAPTER 4

Settlement of collective labour conflicts in Belgium

Jan Rombouts

1 Preliminary remarks

It is useful to recall that Belgium has become a federal state. There are three Regions with some competence in social and economic matters: the Flemish Region, the Walloon Region and the Region of Brussels – the Capital. The Regions have a well-defined territory that is under their jurisdiction. At the same time there are three communities: the Flemish Community, the French speaking Community and the German speaking Community. These communities have some competence in cultural matters and in matters of well-being and personal development. It is important to note that the Communities have no well-defined territory as such, seen in the fact that some parts of the country have a bilingual status.

These remarks on Belgian federalism are important, while the federal structure has an influence on labour relations.

Labour law[1] and also social security belong to the competence of the federal authorities. Considering that the Regions are competent to develop their employment policy, it is easily understood that friction and tensions are possible.

Until now, the basic rules about the organization of labour relations for employees in the public sector also belong to the competence of the federal authorities.[2]

So in Belgium there are at least three 'labour relations systems', one for the private sector, one for the public sector and finally one for the semi-public sector.

2 Characteristics of the Belgian labour relations system for the private sector[3]

2.1 There are no formal tripartite social dialogue bodies in Belgium[4]

This is a first important characteristic of the Belgian labour relations system. The main reason is a historical one. There was an attempt to establish tripartite bodies during the Second World War. After the acceptance of

1 For an overview of Belgian labour law, see Humblet (2004) in French or Humblet (2002) in Dutch.

2 Vande Lanotte (2003), 760 and 970. For an overview of Belgian industrial relations law, see Humblet (2005).

3 For a general overview see Rombouts (2003a).

4 In 1960 a National Committee for Economic Development was created. It had a formal tripartite composition. The Committee has not been called together since the 1970s. It is unclear whether the Committee still exists from a formal legal point of view. Koninklijk besluit van 25 november 1960 tot instelling van een Nationaal Comité voor Economische Expansie (*Belgisch Staatsblad*, 3 november 1960) – Arrêté royal du 25 novembre 1960 portant création d'un Comité national d'expansion économique, (*Moniteur Belge*, 3 novembre 1960).

the Social Pact 1944,[5] bipartism became the rule. At the top level in the social dialogue machinery, there are two important bipartite bodies: a social council the National Labour Council and an economic council, the Central Economic Council. The state is not represented in these councils. Each council is chaired by an independent person.

Since Belgium became a federal state, in the constituent parts of the federation, social and economic councils have been created.[6] But again, they have a bipartite composition and the regional authorities are not represented in the councils.

2.2 Tradition of informal tripartism

Even if there are no tripartite bodies, there is a long-standing tradition of informal tripartite social dialogue in the Belgian labour relations system. Frequently, representatives of the peak organizations of employers and trade unions[7] meet with members of the Inner Cabinet.[8] In that respect Belgium is in full compliance with the principles of ILO-C144 Tripartite Consultation (International Labour Standards) Convention, 1976. At the same time this practice is also an illustration of another characteristic of Belgian labour relations, that is the 'autonomy of the social partners'.

2.3 The autonomy of the social partners

The principle of the autonomy of the social partners is an important element in the application of important international instruments:

- ILO-C87 Freedom of Association and Protection of the Right to Organize Convention, 1948;
- ILO-C98 Right to Organize and Collective Bargaining Convention, 1949;
- ILO-C154 Collective Bargaining Convention, 1981.

There is no interference of the state in matters that concern the organization and action of employers' organizations and trade unions. An important example is that in Belgium trade unions have no corporate capacity: they have no legal personality. However, in some cases the legislator has given them specific rights. For example: the right to represent members in proceedings before a labour court. This principle is at the same time very much linked with the 'principle of subsidiarity'.

---

5 This Social Pact 1944 can be considered as the 'Constitution' of labour relations in Belgium. It is quite different from the recent 'social pacts' in some European countries. See Fajertag (1997).

6 In the Flemish Region, the Walloon Region and the Region of Brussels.

7 Known as the 'Group of Ten', five representatives of the peak organizations of employers and five representatives of the peak organizations of labour.

8 Prime Minister, Deputy Prime Ministers and some other senior members of the Federal Government, *e.g.* the Minister of Labour.

2.4 The principle of subsidiarity

The idea of subsidiarity and the tradition of voluntarism are of major importance in Belgian labour relations. The principle of subsidiarity implies that all matters that can be settled by interested parties are indeed settled by them, without any direct interference of the political authorities.

The Belgian political world generally accepts the principle of subsidiarity concerning social matters. Still, this should not be construed too strictly, as occurred during the period 1980-1986 when an attempt was made by the Belgian Government to pursue a policy of wage restraint. Public authorities imposed a margin for wages negotiations between employers and workers.

An Act on Promotion of Employment and Maintaining Competitiveness[9] was introduced in 1996. The aim was again the introduction of a policy of wage restraint. For the first general bargaining round[10], after the new law came into effect, the government made a formal decision to limit the increase of labour costs during the negotiations for the years 1997-1998.

For the negotiations covering the years 1999-2000, 2001-2002, and 2003-2004, the government accepted the engagement of social partners to comply with a maximum increase in labour costs as recommended by the top-level social partners and did not interfere. Even for the ongoing general bargaining round in 2005-2006, while social partners did not come to a general social policy agreement,[11] the government did not intervene. The government was involved during the results of the – not finalized – negotiations.

This is an example of the wide acceptance of the principle of voluntarism.

Yet, this does not imply that the political authorities are not watching the public interest. More than once, the government has introduced new legislation in absence of a consensus between political decision-makers and social partners.

The government, however, is stimulating collective bargaining in some cases, by subordinating benefits for employers and employees to the conclusion of collective agreements.

2.5 The Belgian labour relations system is an example of a co-ordinated system[12]

The last decades there has been a wide scientific discussion on some elements of labour relations systems. Labour relations in some countries

---

9 Wet van 26 juli 1996 tot bevordering van de werkgelegenheid en tot preventieve vrijwaring van het concurrentievermogen (*Belgisch Staatsblad*, 1 augustus 1996) – Loi du 26 juillet 1996 relative à la promotion de l'emploi et à la sauvegarde préventive de la compétitivité, (*Moniteur Belge*, 1er août 1996).

10 In Belgium every two years collective bargaining takes place in all sectors.

11 *Interprofessioneel Akkoord* (*Centraal Akkoord* in the Netherlands) – *Accord interprofessionnel*. In Belgium these agreements are not regarded as a 'social pact' or as a 'collective agreement'.

12 Rombouts (1996) 30-44.

have been described as 'centralized' and others as 'decentralized'. The most important indicator was the level where key collective bargaining takes place: at the national level or at enterprise level. But, as always, there are intermediate types. Belgium is an example of the latter case: there is a co-ordinated system of collective bargaining. There is a kind of division of labour between the national level, the level of branches of industry (sectoral level) and the enterprise level.

2.6 The Belgian labour relations system is a dynamic system

One can distinguish two kinds of collective bargaining systems.[13] In fact it is more about two types of bargaining procedures. They are distinguishable as types, but there are many overlaps and hybrid forms. One is sometimes referred to as the institutional or dynamic method, the other as the contractual or static method.

The institutional method (dynamic system) consists in the creation of one or more permanent bilateral bodies. "They are known as a joint industrial council, a conciliation board, or a joint committee, on which both sides are represented by an equal number of members, sometimes (in a minority of cases) with an independent chairman presiding".[14] It is said that – at that time – the institutional method was widespread in the United Kingdom, Belgium being the country that is (was) most similar to Britain.

In the contractual method, the actors come together, negotiate, arrive at an agreement and then disperse. From time to time they meet as the need arises, *i.e.* when the agreement is coming to an end and they wish to renew the agreement.

2.7 The importance of collective bargaining in Belgian labour relations

Collective bargaining as a 'rule-making process' is of paramount importance in Belgian labour relations. Collective agreements can be concluded at different levels: national and intersectoral, sectoral and at the level of the enterprise.

Collective agreements concluded within the legal framework that is set up by government (joint bodies), have a quasi-automatic extension or coverage. All employers and workers are bound by the collective agreement for normative or substantive individual rights. The binding of such collective agreements can even become more pressing, when they are, at the request of the social partners, declared to be binding, *erga omnes* by a Royal Order. The non-observance of their clauses becomes in that case a criminal offence.

---

13 Kahn-Freund (1983) 70-74.

14 *Ibid.*, 70.

One could say that from time to time there is some friction or some kind of competition between social partners and government in the field of law making concerning labour matters.

2.8 Institutional framework for collective bargaining in the private sector

2.8.1 At the central level

At the central level, a bipartite National Labour Council[15] has been established. Initially, the Council was intended to be the top-level advisory body on all social matters. This is still a very important mission, since the government has to seek the opinion of the Council on all draft social legislation or draft government regulations.[16] Since the Collective Agreements Act of 1968[17] came into effect, the Council is considered by law as a 'joint body' and collective agreements can be concluded within it. In most cases these collective agreements are intended to have economy-wide scope.

The National Labour Council has 26 members, representing both sides of industry. It has an independent Chairman and a Secretary-General who is responsible for management and the staff of the Council.

Therefore the National Labour Council can be seen as 1) a consultative body, 2) a joint body and 3) an administrative body as far it concerns its internal affairs.[18]

At the central level, there is also a Central Economic Council.[19] It is not strictly bipartite, because consumers' representatives and some independent experts also have seats in the Council. The Council is the top-level advisory body on all economic matters. There is an informal but strong co-ordination of the work of both Councils.

---

15 Wet van 29 mei 1952 tot inrichting van de Nationale Arbeidsraad, (*Belgisch Staatsblad*, 31 mei 1952) – Loi organique du 29 mai 1952 du Conseil national du travail, loi du 29 mai 1952, (*Moniteur Belge*, 31 mai 1952).

16 Rombouts (1976), 53.

17 Wet van 5 december 1968 betreffende de collectieve arbeidsovereenkomsten en de paritaire comités (*Belgisch Staatsblad*, 15 januari 1969) – Loi du 5 décembre 1968 sur les conventions collectives de travail et les commissions paritaires, (*Moniteur Belge*, 15 janvier 1969).

18 Rombouts (1976), 112.

19 Wet van 20 september 1948 houdende organisatie van het bedrijfsleven (*Belgisch Staatsblad*, 27-28 september 1948) – Loi du 20 septembre 1948 portant organisation de l'économie (*Moniteur Belge*, 27-28 septembre 1948).

2.8.2 At sectoral level (branches of industry) – joint committees

At industry level, the government can, at the request of the social partners or on its own initiative, establish bipartite (sectoral) joint committees.[20] As a general rule, collective agreements concluded in a joint committee apply to the whole industry within their jurisdiction. If a joint committee so wishes, it can request that the government establishes one or more joint subcommittees, thereby providing an opportunity to engage in sub-sectoral collective bargaining. Collective agreements concluded in a joint subcommittee apply to all employers of the industry subsector concerned.

The government appoints the members on the recommendation of employers and trade unions. First, the Federal Minister of Labour decides on the distribution of seats between the eligible organizations. Only the most representative organizations receive one or more seats in the Committee.

Determination of membership is of paramount importance for organizations, given the fact that the conclusion of a collective agreement in a joint committee is subject to the approval of the draft agreement by each organization holding a seat.

It is now a generally accepted practise that *Sociaal Bemiddelaars/Conciliateurs Sociaux* (Labour Conciliators-Mediators being members of the Labour Relations Office) are appointed as chairperson and vice-chairperson of the joint committees, while other officials from the Labour Relations Office are in charge of the secretariat for the committees[21].

The four statutory missions of the joint committees are:[22]

1. to encourage the conclusion of collective agreements;
2. to prevent and to settle labour disputes;

Usually the joint committees set up a conciliation board for this purpose. It is a characteristic of the Belgian labour relations system that the settlement of labour disputes is part of the collective bargaining process and that it can be a rule-making process as well.

3. to give advice to Parliament, the Cabinet, the National Labour Council and the Central Economic Council; and
4. to carry out any other task assigned to them by law or by the above-mentioned bodies.

However, since the 1970s the role of joint committees is steadily growing[23] and they intervene in various ways in the elaboration of labour law.[24]

---

[20] Rombouts (1972), 1189-1222; Rombouts (1976) 20, and Collective Agreements Act (1968), Article 35.

[21] Rombouts (1993) 241-246.

[22] Collective Agreements Act (1968), Article 38.

[23] Rombouts (1990), 181-214.

[24] Rombouts (2005b), in: Rombouts (2005a).

2.9 Conciliation and mediation in collective labour disputes

Complex conciliation-mediation machinery has been set up. As labour and management see themselves as lawmakers, they are strongly engaged in the settlement of labour disputes through the process of conciliation and mediation. Social partners actively participate in the machinery of conciliation boards, while a labour conciliator-mediator (from the Ministry of Labour) chairs the proceedings. The very active role of social partners is a consequence of the characteristics of the Belgian labour relations system.

3 Characteristics of the Belgian labour relations system for the public sector

3.1 The situation before 1980

For a long time, there has been a tradition of information and consultation in the field of public sector labour relations. Under the influence of French administrative law,[25] which was introduced in Belgium, public employees are in a subordinate position regulated by statute law. Eventually it is the public authority that will decide unilaterally on the 'position' of public employees. For employees working in the public sector with a common contract of employment, the situation is not clear at all. However, the government and the public sector trade unions also have been engaged for a long time in negotiations leading to a 'collective agreement'[26]. In legal terms these kinds of agreements have only a moral authority and are not legally binding.

3.2 The situation after 1980

The Labour Relations (Public Sector) Act 1974[27] formalized collective bargaining, consultation and information in the public sector. First of all this act set up a general framework for collective labour relations in the public sector:

---

[25] For the French approach, see Neville Brown (1998) 40.

[26] Not a 'collective agreement' as meant in the Collective Agreements Act 1968 (private sector).

[27] Wet van 19 december 1974 tot regeling van de betrekkingen tussen de overheden en de vakbonden van haar personeel (*Belgisch Staatsblad*, 4 december 1974), Loi du 19 décembre 1974 organisant les relations entre les autorités publiques et les syndicats des agents relevant de ces autorités (*Moniteur Belge*, 24 décembre 1974).

Organization: institutions for bargaining and concertation

1°) Bargaining committees

- a general bargaining committee for the whole public sector, that is Committee A;
- a general bargaining committee for the federal administration, that is Committee B;
- a general bargaining committee for the regional administrations, that is Committee C;
- bargaining committees for each 'sector' (*e.g.* Committee XI for the federal administration in the field of social affairs) to be defined after bargaining in Committee B.

It is clear that this system is inspired by the collective bargaining structure of the private sector. The major change, introduced by the Labour Relations (Public Sector) Act 1974, was that a process of collective bargaining has to be engaged in by the public authority, before a decision can be made. It should be a real negotiation and not a simple information or opinion seeking one from public sector trade unions. It is fair to say that the public authority has the 'duty to bargain in good faith'. The result of this process is put in a 'protocole'.

The *Raad van State/Conseil d'État* (High Administrative Court) can review the negotiation process and can annul administrative decisions if the authority only organized a *pro forma* bargaining.

Scope of collective bargaining

a) basic rules about administrative status, payment, pensions, labour relations and the organization of welfare services. The government can only decide what 'basic rules' means, after going through a collective bargaining process;
b) regulations about the organization of work and working time. But again, the government can only decide about these regulations after going through a collective bargaining process.

Draft legislation, on the initiative of the government, can only be sent to Parliament after being submitted for negotiation to the appropriate bargaining committee. It should be noted that this Act of Parliament also applies to public employees with a contract of employment. However, the attitude of the government in this matter can be criticized.

2°) Concertation committees

Concertation Committees are to be established for each administrative unit within federal administration. There should be concertation not only about all matters that are considered as being no 'basic rules of the Public Service', but also about organization of work and workings hours in a specific situation. The committees are also competent in matters such as human relations in the public services and for matters concerning productivity.

In the public sector, Concertation Committees also have tasks that are comparable to the mission, which in the private sector are attributed to the Committee for Prevention and Well-being at Work.[28]

Extension of the system introduced by the Labour Relations (Public Sector) Act 1974

The Labour Relations (Public Sector) Act 1974 has been an example for the establishment of labour relations systems in others parts of the public sector, such as the former *Gendarmerie* (National Police),[29] the Military,[30] the unified Police Force[31] and most recently for operative agents of the National Security Service.[32]

4 Labour relations in the semi-public sector or the semi-private sector

An Act of 1991[33] introduced a specific labour relations system for public enterprises. Rather confusingly, this Act introduced the system of a 'joint committee' in each public enterprise, which has a mission comparable to a works council and/or a Health and Safety Committee in the private sector.[34]

A 'General Committee for public enterprises' should perform tasks comparable to the general bargaining committee for the whole public sector (Committee A) as arranged for in the Labour Relations (Public Sector) Act 1974. Since few matters seem to be of a common interest to all of the public enterprises, the impact of this bargaining unit is questionable.

A process of privatization is going on in these public enterprises. In the (far) future there should be only two separate labour relations systems (private and public sector). In practice, one can see that during the privatization process there is a clear tendency to maintain some, more favourable rules for the public enterprises.

In this sector no specific machinery for conciliation or mediation exists.

---

[28] These are the former 'Safety and Health Committees'.

[29] Act of 11 July 1978 (*Belgisch Staatsblad – Moniteur Belge*, 18 August 1978), amended by Acts of 10 February 1998 and of 25 March 1998.

[30] A separate Act was passed on the same day, Act of 11 July 1978 (*Belgisch Staatsblad – Moniteur Belge*, 18 August 1978).

[31] Act of 24 March 1999 (*Belgisch Staatsblad – Moniteur Belge*, 8 May 1999).

[32] Act of 17 March 2004 (*Belgisch Staatsblad – Moniteur Belge*, 2 April 2004).

[33] Wet van 21 maart 1991 betreffende de hervorming van sommige economische overheidsbedrijven (*Belgisch Staatsblad*, 27 maart 1991) – Loi du 21 mars 1991 portant réforme de certaines entreprises publiques économiques (*Moniteur Belge*, 27 mars 1991).

[34] Jacqmain (1992), 185.

5 Machinery for the settlement of labour disputes in the private sector[35]

5.1 Dispute procedures in collective agreements

The social peace clause

In some countries, like for example Belgium, it is considered that every collective labour agreement contains a 'social peace clause' even if this clause is not explicitly mentioned. This is a consequence of the contractual nature of a collective agreement. All parties have to execute and apply the contract in good faith – *pacta sunt servanda*. The peace obligation ends when the collective agreement expires.[36]

This question is far from theoretic and Belgian negotiators, in most cases, do mention in their collective agreements that both parties are satisfied with the results of the bargaining process and that during the term of the agreement they will not formulate demands on all matters that are regulated in the agreement. Difficulties in relation to the execution and application of the collective agreement will be submitted to negotiations or to conciliation or mediation. In some cases there are also clauses stating that at the end of term of the agreement, before any industrial action commences, parties have to formulate proposals for a (re)new(ed) agreement.

However, in various cases some problems are not resolved:

- What should be done if an employer does not comply with an obligation of statutory labour law?
- What should be done if the employer refuses to apply the clauses of the collective agreement, or is applying the agreement in a way that is not correct?
- What should be done if a new issue, not covered by a previous agreement, is becoming very urgent and the employer refuses to engage in negotiations?

Procedural clauses in collective agreements[37]

It is not uncommon that the collective agreement itself contains clauses about the procedure that has to be followed in case of a labour dispute:

- a labour dispute first has to be examined at the company level. It is accepted that both union and management may call for the assistance of representatives of their workers' or their employers' organization;
- in case of a labour dispute, the question must be submitted to an *ad hoc* reconciliation committee at the local level;
- the sectoral conciliation board has to meet as soon as possible, in difficult cases even the same day (for example, the docks industry);

[35] See De Roo (1994) and Valdés Dal-Ré (2003).

[36] Salomon (2000), 476.

[37] Rombouts (2003) in: Rigaux (2003).

- the sectoral conciliation board has to meet within 48 hours maximum (some local arrangements in the metalworking industry);
- unions engage to support only industrial action that is put in motion by their responsible officers;
- prior notice should be given before industrial action takes place (in many cases 7 days);
- industrial action without following the procedural clauses will lead to the non-payment by the employer to the sectoral social fund that reimburses a part of the union fee to unionized workers (union bonus) or that finances trade union training.

Clause about the appointment of a mediator

In some collective agreements, there is a clause that states that a mediator shall be appointed for the term of the agreement or that a mediator shall be appointed in case of necessity. This is the case in agreements at the enterprise level that are, from the point of view of the law, not to be considered as collective agreements[38].

This seems to be a more common approach in countries with the common law tradition and indeed it happens in foreign-based companies.

5.2 Formal machinery at the sectoral level – the conciliation boards

One of the statutory missions of a joint committee is to provide conciliation and mediation services. As has been mentioned before, collective bargaining and conciliation-mediation is seen as being part of one and the same social process. This opinion is even more underlined by the fact that the Chair of nearly every joint committee is appointed from the members of the Conciliation-Mediation Division of the Labour Relations Office. These government officials are chosen for their specific knowledge of social and economic matters and perform their duties as a Chair (or a Vice-Chair) in their capacity of an expert in social and economic affairs.

It is fair to say that the fact that professional conciliators-mediators are appointed to chair the joint committees clearly indicates the intention of the Federal Government to promote some form of 'preventive conciliation'. In their day-to-day business, the Chair is acting as an independent and neutral expert. It is clear, however, that he or she can already collect important information in that stage, which can be very useful when, later on, a labour conflict arises.

Every joint committee can decide to create a 'conciliation board' to deal with the mission to prevent and to settle labour disputes. The conciliation board is in fact a standing working party of the joint committee and is also chaired by the Chair of the committee. In most cases a limited number of members of the

---

[38] As, *i.e.* the agreement is not registered with the Labour Relations Office.

joint committee assist the meeting. In many cases those members are in fact the spokespeople of the various organizations represented in the joint committee.

The conciliation board works under the rules that are laid down by the joint committee. The procedure applied is generally as follows: in the conciliation board sits at least one representative of each organization represented in the joint committee. Sometimes it is considered sufficient that there is a delegate of each trade union that has membership at the level of the enterprise concerned.[39]

Therefore, in the conciliation board a strict parity between the numbers of delegates is not required. This is the consequence of the board's rules on decision-making. In the conciliation board unions and employer's organizations play the major role. The delegations of employers and workers, as such, are of equal importance and unanimity of all organizations is required to address a recommendation to the disputing parties.

The conciliation board will hold a hearing where the parties concerned can explain their point of view. The party that requested the conciliation will speak first, the chair and the members of the conciliation board will listen to the parties and they can ask for more information. They should refrain from giving any indication about their opinion during the hearing.

Then the chairperson will adjourn the hearing and will withdraw with the members of the conciliation board to deliberate the case. It often happens that members of the conciliation board, with the consent of the board, have unofficial talks with the party they represent. In this way the chances of success of a draft recommendation can be checked before it is officially put forward.

If the conciliation board reaches an understanding, this is announced to the disputing parties, when the hearing is resumed, as a formal recommendation. As has been mentioned, it is possible that the recommendation states that the case is to be sent back to the enterprise level. It even happens that the conciliation board desires that the results of these new talks be reported back to the conciliation board or to the chair.

The disputing parties are under no obligation to accept the conciliation board's recommendation, but practice shows that they usually do.

Yet, if the conciliation board is unable to reach an understanding, it then can happen that the chairperson of the conciliation board makes a recommendation. This is announced as such and can take occur in a situation where, for some reason related to the techniques of negotiation, the proposal cannot be officially accepted by all organizations. In the conciliation board nobody is openly or formally opposed. This is the typical way of consensus decision-making.

However, it can happen that no solution at all is reached. Then, either this fact is stated officially and announced when the hearing is resumed, or the chairperson of the conciliation board can decide to make a further attempt to bring parties together. Here he will then act in his capacity of a labour concili-

[39] In this situation, the conciliation-mediation proceedings cannot end with the conclusion of a collective agreement at sectoral level.

ator-mediator. There is no straightforward answer to the question whether it is opportune to do so, and at what moment it may be done. It has everything to do with the experience of the labour conciliator-mediator. He can either continue negotiating with the members of the conciliation board, in which case he will make clear his point of view, or he can choose to adjourn the meeting of the conciliation board and meet with each party privately.

The labour conciliator-mediator can also make a personal recommendation to the disputing parties. But this is then under his/her own responsibility.

As a result of this process, in many cases social partners decide to adapt or adjust collective agreements that have been under discussion. A new agreement can be concluded if the problems that were discussed were not already regulated by collective agreement.

Results of conciliation-mediation

The result of a conciliation-mediation meeting can be:

- the formal statement that (re)conciliation is (at that moment) not possible;
- a non-committal recommendation of the person or persons that have acted as conciliators-mediators, whereby a solution of the conflict is suggested to parties. In some cases this happens as a draft collective agreement;
- a non-committal recommendation of the person or persons that have acted as conciliators-mediators, whereby a solution of the conflict is proposed to the parties, with the suggestion to submit the proposed solution to a ballot;
- a non-committal recommendation of the person or persons that have acted as conciliators-mediators, whereby it is suggested to the parties to continue or to start discussions in other conditions (back to company level, restarting negations after a cooling off period);
- the conclusion of a new collective agreement;
- the formal announcement of an interpretation of a collective agreement.

Excursus: conciliation-mediation beyond the sectoral level

In some special cases, when all attempts fail, it can happen that the Minister of Employment and Labour appoints one or several labour conciliator-mediator(s) to handle the problem. Examples are the appointment, in a dispute that very deeply affected an automobile assembly factory, of a commission composed of three conciliator-mediators or the appointment of two labour conciliator-mediators in a dispute that paralyzed a steel company. These exceptional measures are taken by the Minister, on the advice or after consultation with the Director General of the Labour Relations Office.

Until now only one case is known where the Minister ordered the Director General of the Labour Relations Office to undertake an 'inquiry' into the deeper causes of a lasting labour dispute.

5.3 Conciliation-mediation techniques at enterprise level

At enterprise level, if parties so desire, there is always the possibility to engage in collective bargaining. Under Belgian labour law, there has to be a works council in enterprises with more than 100 employees and also a Heath and Safety Committee in enterprises with more than 50 employees. In both cases, these are bipartite bodies with an equal representation of the employer and the employees. The representatives of the employees are elected every four years. The employer of course appoints his representatives in those bodies. The main tasks are in the field of information, consultation and social dialogue in general. However, in the Belgian way of seeing things, these bodies are not considered for collective bargaining as such.

Collective bargaining at the enterprise level takes place between the employer and unions. However in those enterprises where formal 'trade union representatives' have been recognized, they are partners at the bargaining table. The institution of 'trade union representatives' has not been created by statute law, but by framework-collective agreements concluded in the National Labour Council. Every joint committee has the faculty to decide by collective agreement about the whole set of rights and duties of the trade union representatives[40]. In any case the trade union representatives have rights and duties in the following areas:

- promotion of good labour relations;
- representation/assistance of employees in grievance procedures;
- monitoring the correct implementation of labour law and collective agreements;
- prevention and settlement of labour disputes.

However, when trade union representatives engage in collective bargaining, they are obliged to call in union officials when the conclusion of a collective agreement is considered. Under Belgian law, one or more union officials should indeed sign the collective agreement.

When a labour dispute arises at the enterprise level, and if trade union representatives are appointed, the employer should, as a good practice or under the clauses of an applicable collective agreement, have one or more conciliation meetings with these union representatives. In many cases, the employer can bring in external expertise to these conciliation meetings (*e.g.* consultants from the employers' association), as is also the case for the trade union side (union officials).

It can happen that these conciliation-mediation proceedings at the enterprise level are put into the sectoral collective agreements that have to be applied in the enterprise. In some sectors, it may happen that even at this stage, employers' organizations and unions that are represented in the joint committee act as hosts for these conciliation meetings.

40 Rigaux (2001).

It can also happen that conciliation-mediation proceedings are taking place under the direction of a labour conciliator-mediator from the Labour Relations Office. As a general rule, this happens only after the case has been brought before the conciliation board of the joint committee and a decision is reached whereby the case is sent back to the enterprise level.

In really exceptional cases, it may occur that, because of the nature of the dispute, a labour conciliator-mediator from the Labour Relations Office is immediately in charge of the case without proceedings before the conciliation board. The labour conciliator-mediator only deals with the employer and with the union officials, not with individual employees

5.4 The role of the Labour Relations Office[41]

In Belgian labour relations, although the government is considered to have only a complementary role in this field, the Ministry of Labour has several duties concerning these matters. The Labour Relations Office is the branch of the department that is responsible for conciliation and mediation services and for assisting the social partners in their collective bargaining process at sectoral level (including the work of the conciliation boards). The Office is of also in charge of all administrative formalities concerning collective agreements that are concluded at all different levels, that is registration.

Actually, the Conciliation and Mediation Division is composed of 4 senior labour conciliator-mediators, 13 labour conciliator-mediators and 11 associate labour conciliator-mediators. In Belgium the Minister of Labour is politically responsible for maintaining social peace. It is therefore not surprising that each labour conciliator-mediator, in performing his particular duties, directly reports to the Minister of Labour.

6 Absence of machinery for the settlement of labour disputes in the public sector

Most striking is the complete absence of machinery for conciliation and mediation in the public sector. Exceptions are the labour relations for operative agents of the National Security Service. In this case, there is a separate chapter dealing with conciliation or mediation in the Act of 17 March 2004.

---

41 Since a recent reorganisation, the Labour Relations Office has now become the Directorate of Collective Labour Relations.

6.1 General rule: no conciliation-mediation machinery is established

It may be amazing, but as a general rule there are no provisions about conciliation-mediation machinery in the public sector. It seems rather difficult to include Ministers in a conciliation-mediation procedure, especially if the conciliator-mediator is a public official. Labour disputes in the public sector are, in practise, settled through direct negotiations between representatives of the public authority concerned[42] and of representatives of public sector trade unions.

6.2 Exceptions

An exception to this general rule is found in the Labour Relations (National Security Service) Act 2004.[43] This Act has a chapter on Conciliation-Mediation, that is articles 17 to 22.

The first consideration is that the right to strike is incompatible with the status of operative agents of the National Security Service[44]

A Ministerial Committee, with the consent of trade unions, appoints a conciliator-mediator. The conciliator-mediator has to call for a conciliation-mediation meeting when this is requested by at least two trade unions or by the government. This meeting has to take place no longer than seven days after receiving a request and the ministers should attend in person the conciliation-mediation meeting. The conciliator-mediator drafts the minutes of the meeting. If no settlement is reached, the conciliator-mediator has to submit the minutes of the conciliation-mediation meeting, with his opinion, to the Ministers concerned. The Council of Ministers has to take into consideration the case in the next meeting.

A second exception is the French-speaking Radio and Television Corporation (*RTBF*). The Decree of the French Community establishing this public corporation provides for a labour relations system close to the system of the semi-public sector, but it also provides for the appointment of a conciliator-mediator. The conciliator-mediator is chosen from the members of the Conciliation-Mediation Division of the Labour Relations Office. The Federal Minister of Labour has appointed, with the consent of the Minister of the French Community in charge of radio and television, two members to serve as conciliator-mediator and substitute conciliator-mediator.

---

42 *E.g.* members of the Political Office of a Minister.

43 Act of 17 March 2004 *(Belgisch Staatsblad – Moniteur Belge*, 2 April 2004).

44 This means that staff of the central administration of the National Security Service has the right to strike.

7 The right to strike

7.1 The private sector

For years, Belgian law had no provisions concerning the right to strike. After some time the classical interpretation became that the employment contract was suspended and that there was no breach of contract.

The Belgian *Hof van Cassatie/Cour de Cassation* (Supreme Court), however, decided that the right to strike exists, now that Parliament has adopted legislation concerning essential supplies and services in the case of a 'collective stoppage of work' or of a 'lock out' (Essential Supplies and Services in Peacetime Act – 1948).[45]

Although from a strict legal point of view there are no specific rules about the strike phenomenon, the 1948 legislation prescribes what measures ought to be taken when a collective stoppage of work of a lock out is expected.

These 'measures' are to be prepared by management and labour in the framework of their joint committee. Every joint committee, for the sector under its jurisdiction, is to make up a list of all the essential supplies and services that have to be assured in the case of a labour conflict. The joint committees have to take a 'decision' on this issue. It is well understood that in that case, and contrary to the decision-making process in the case of a collective agreement, it is the joint committee as a public body that has to take the decision.[46] In the case of the conclusion of a collective agreement, it is the trade unions and employers' organizations that agree on a draft-agreement and not the joint committee as such.

A decision of a public body, in this case a decision taken with a majority of 75% of labour and of management's representatives in the joint committee, is from a legal point of view almost akin to an administrative decision in the sense of administrative law.[47] The decision of the joint committee has to be given a binding *erga omnes* effect through a Royal Order, otherwise there is no legal effect.

However, in this case the role of the government is not limited to the choice to accept or to refuse the decision as it is the case for collective agreements. The government can determine the list of essential supplies and services, after sending a warning to the joint committee concerned, after having sought the opinion of the National Labour Council and after a Royal Order in Council has been taken containing in detail the motivation for this action. This system has been criticized in Parliament during the debates before the final voting. The argument was that in this matter it was clearly an issue for the government itself,

---

45 Wet van 19 augustus 1948 betreffende de prestaties van algemeen belang in vredestijd (*Belgisch Staatsblad*, 2 juli 1948) – Loi du 19 août 1948 relative aux prestations d'intérêt public en temps de paix, (*Moniteur Belge*, 21 août 1948), as amended in 1963.

46 Rombouts (2003) in: Rigaux (2003) 87-136.

47 Rombouts (1976), 86-87; and Rombouts (2005b) in: Rombouts (2005a).

and it should not have been left to social partners acting in a joint committee.[48] Most joint committees haven taken on this responsibility and have fixed a list of essential supplies and services.

The next step in the implementation of this legislation is that in the case of a labour conflict, the law requires that social partners themselves take the responsibility to implement the law and regulations. This is to be done through a working party that is created within the joint committee. This working party should take all measures so that the list of essential supplies and services is respected.

There is, however, a problem in Belgian labour legislation. Belgium has, after years of hesitation, finally ratified the European Social Charter of 1961.[49] Since the ratification of the European Social Charter the right to strike has become part of the Belgian national law system. The European Social Charter stipulates that the right to strike may only be limited:

- through obligations that may arise out of collective agreements previously entered into (Article 6, section 4);
- when prescribed by law and necessary in a democratic society for the protection of the rights and freedoms of others or for the protection of public interests, national security, public health or morals. These restrictions shall not be applied for any purpose other than that for which they have been prescribed (Article 31).

The definition or better the lack of a clear definition of essential supplies and services in the Belgian situation makes it rather complicated. Indeed, one could make a distinction between 'minimum services and supplies' and 'essential services and supplies'[50].

In the former case, one can think about a whole series of measures on which social partners agree (by collective agreement) what services should be maintained in their common interest. So maintenance of a steel mill or a glass mill is important, both for labour and management. Therefore one may suppose that after a labour conflict the aim of all actors is to start up normal operations immediately. If, in between, the steel mill or the glass mill was not maintained, this would be not acceptable, as then infrastructure would be destroyed.

In the second case, one can think about a whole series of measures that in any event should be taken in the general interest. If social partners would be unable to take these measures, it would then be the duty of the public authority to impose them.

---

48 Parlementaire Documenten, Kamer van Volksvertegenwoordigers 1962-1963, 4 april 1963 – Documents parlementaires, Chambre des Représentants, 1962-1963, 4 avril 1963.

49 Wet van 11 juli 1990 houdende goedkeuring van het Europees Sociaal Charter en de Bijlagen, gedaan te Turijn op 18 oktober 1961 (*Belgisch Staatsblad*, 28 december 1990) – Loi du 11 juillet 1990 portant approbation de la Charte Sociale Européenne et de l'Annexe faites à Turin le 18 octobre 1961, (*Moniteur Belge*, 28 décembre 1990.

50 Rombouts (2003b) 97-88.

But this distinction between minimum services and essential services is not very well elaborated in Belgian labour law. It will be a challenge to put order in this issue,[51] since it is both in the interest of labour and management to have clear rules about what has to be done in the case of a labour conflict. For public authorities, it is important to be able to make up an efficient plan for those cases where labour (or management) is not following the rules.

On the other hand, it is important to see that social partners in their day-to-day practice have, in a large number of cases, decided upon some rules that have to be respected in the case of a labour conflict. This is of course positive, but it is important to mention that these 'arrangements' are not taken in the framework of the Essential Supplies and Services in Peacetime Act (1948), but in the framework of the Collective Agreements Act (1968).

It seems that, without doubt, the actual situation in Belgium is no longer in compliance with the viewpoint of the experts that monitor the application of the European Social Charter.[52]

7.2 The public sector

Since the 1950s, there is a 'de facto' acceptance of strikes in the public sector. But, as is the case in the private sector, there is no appropriate legislation. For many years the formal recognition of the right to strike for public employees has been an obstacle for ratifying the European Social Charter.

In the public sector, there is not a system that is comparable to the Essential Supplies and Services in Peacetime Act – 1948, that only applies to the private sector.[53] From a formal point of view, the right to strike in the public sector is to be found in the European Social Charter, as this legal instrument is now part of the Belgian legal order.

In practise, the right to strike is beyond discussion in the public sector, taking into account some limitations introduced by statutory law. This is the case for military personnel, when they are involved in an operation.

8 Prospects for the future

8.1 The private sector

The implementation of the Essential Supplies and Services in Peacetime Act 1948 is bound by the acceptance of social partners of the basic rules of this legislation. Although this still is the case, it should be noted that,

51 About essential services, see M. Rigaux (2003a), 25, who pleads for a review of the definitions of 1945 and also Morris (1986).

52 T. Jaspers (2003) in: Rigaux (2003a) 53-54.

53 It should be noted that public authorities have tried to apply the principles of that legislation in the public sector, without any legal funding.

for several years, most sector joint committees have failed to update the list of essential supplies and services in their jurisdiction. Some more recently established committees have not even formulated a preparatory 'decision'. Evidently, this situation should be reversed, as the existing system is a guarantee of the exercise of the right to strike. However, one can see that the social partners are ready to agree, in collective agreements, about some procedural aspects in the case of a labour conflict.

The message should be clear: it is necessary to update statutory law and regulations concerning this matter.

Excursus: the (changing) role of the judiciary

The issue of a collective labour conflict, as such, cannot be brought before a court of law. The Labour Courts are only competent in conflicts between an individual employee and employeur. In the Labour Courts, there are professional judges and lay judges. Typically a Chamber in a Labour Court consists of one professional judge, presiding, and of two lay judges representing each side of industry.

The competence of the Labour Courts is restricted to labour law and social security matters.

However, other courts in the judiciary system can intervene, that is when unlawful acts are committed in the context of a labour conflict. This has become a delicate matter in the recent years and some rulings of judges have been criticized, not only by trade unionists but also by academics and recently by the Committee of Experts that is set up to monitor the application of the European Social Charter.

It is indeed difficult to defend that a judge can forbid some forms of industrial action, referring to the existence of a 'grand danger' if a strike takes place. This is the influence of the introduction of a system of 'pre-trial conciliation' for individual labour conflicts. Recently the Belgian legislator has introduced a (re)new(ed) system of pre-trial conciliation-mediation in the case of individual labour conflicts.[54]

As has been mentioned before, in many cases, the social partners in sectoral conciliation boards do not make a systematic difference between various kinds of labour conflicts. However, it seems inevitable that in many cases management in many sectors will refuse in the future to take into consideration individual labour conflicts in meetings of a conciliation board.

Until now it was not uncommon to conciliate and mediate in individual labour conflicts, as frequently these conflicts covered in fact collective labour conflicts.

---

[54] Adaptation of 'Gerechtelijk wetboek– Code judicaire' by Act of Parliament, 21 February 2005 (*Belgisch Staatsblad – Moniteur Belge*, 22 March 2005). See X (2005).

8.2 The public sector

It is clear that there is a need in the public sector for a system of voluntary limitation of the right to strike. Considering the fact that in the public sector there is no legal funding for 'collective agreements' this serves as an excuse for not facing the problem. When a strike occurs in the public sector, it is to be noted that from time to time a private bill is introduced in Parliament, seeking to set up a system comparable to the Essential Supplies and Services in Peacetime Act 1948.

It may be hoped that one day there will be a breakthrough in the attitudes of trade unions and public authorities. As is the case in the private sector, there is a tendency among the judiciary to intervene.

9 Evaluation and concluding remarks

There is a long-standing tradition in Belgium in the field of conciliation and mediation. It is generally seen as a good practice to submit labour disputes to conciliation-mediation.

An important characteristic is that social partners themselves accept a major role in the process of conciliation and mediation, which guarantees in most cases a result that satisfies both parties.

The Labour Conciliator-Mediators of the Labour Relations Office have a very important role, as chair of joint committees and as chair of conciliation boards. From time to time, they act as Conciliator-Mediator under their own responsibility. In difficult labour disputes, the Labour Relations Office will not rest and, in an ongoing way, will try to be an intermediary between the parties in dispute.

The Belgian labour relations system offers a remedy for labour disputes that is fully in line with the philosophy of the ILO recommendations. The proceedings are easy to access, open to all and free of charge.

The fact that there is a kind of 'preventive mediation', as conciliators-mediators are chairing negotiations at the sectoral level (joint committees) and, if the needs arise at the conciliation-mediation proceeding (conciliation board), insures that the system is performing well. In some difficult labour disputes, a 'role conflict' can arise. Generally speaking, it is favourable that the conciliator-mediator knows the traditions and practices of a given sector. In exceptional cases, it can be better to bring in another conciliator-mediator, who assists or takes over the case. This remains a delicate matter.

It is amazing – frustating – also for Belgian labour relations experts, to see that the conciliation and mediation machinery is almost unknown in the semi-public and public sectors. Until now no professional body exists for conciliators-mediators. This could change due to the renewed introduction of pre-trial conciliation-mediation.

Bibliography (which in fact is only a list of works that are cited in the text)

BAINBRIDGE (2002)
T. Bainbridge, *The Penguin Companion to European Union*, London, PenguinBooks, 3rd Ed., 2002

DE ROO (1994)
A. J. De Roo and R. W. Jagtenberg, *Settling Labour Disputes in Europe*, PhD-diss., Erasmus University Rotterdam, 1994

FAJERTAG (1997)
G. Fajertag and Ph. Pochet, *Social Pacts in Europe, Brussels*, ETUI, 1997

HUMBLET (2005)
P. Humblet and M. Rigaux, *Belgian Industrial Relations Law*, Antwerpen-Oxford, Intersentia, 2005

HUMBLET (2004)
P. Humblet and M. Rigaux (ed.), *Aperçu du droit du travail belge*, Bruxelles, Bruylant, 2004

HUMBLET (2002)
P. Humblet and M. Rigaux (ed.), *Synopsis van het Belgisch Arbeidsrecht*, Antwerpen-Groningnen, Intersentia, 2002

JACQMAIN (1992)
J. Jacqmain, 'Le statut du personnel des entreprises publiques', in: *Les Entreprises Publiques Autonomes*, Bruxelles, Bruylant, 1992

JASPERS (2003)
T. Jaspers, 'Het vitale belang van het recht op collectieve acties. Een verkenning van de jurisprudentie van het Europees Comité van Sociale Rechten naar reikwijdte van het recht op collectieve acties', in: M. Rigaux and F. Dorssemont (ed.), *Vitale behoeften, essentiële diensten, minimumprestaties en stakingsrecht*, Antwerpen-Groningen, Intersentia, 2003, 27-54

KAHN-FREUND (1983)
O. Kahn-Freund, *Labour and the Law*, ed. by P. Davies and M. Freedland, 3rd ed., London, Stevens and Sons, 1983

MORRIS (1986)
G. Morris, *Strikes in Essential Services*, London-New York, Mansell Publishing, 1986

NEVILLE BROWN (1998)
L. Neville Brown and J. S. Bell, *French Administrative Law*, Oxford; Clarendon Press, 5th ed., 1998

RIGAUX (2003a)
M. Rigaux and F. Dorssemont (ed.), *Vitale behoeften, essentiële diensten, minimumprestaties en stakingsrecht*, Antwerpen-Groningen, Intersentia, 2003

RIGAUX (2003b)
M. Rigaux, 'Naar een amendering en een actualisering van de Prestatiewet?', in: M. Rigaux and F. Dorssemont (ed.) *Vitale behoeften, essentiële diensten, minimumprestaties en stakingsrecht*, 2003, 1-26

RIGAUX (2001)
M. Rigaux, and P. Humblet (ed.), *Syndicale afvaardiging of de sociale tegenmacht in de onderneming : knelpunten i.v.m. het statuut*, Antwerpen, Intersentia, 2001
RIGAUX (1990)
M. Rigaux, (ed.), *Actuele problemen van het arbeidsrecht 3*, Antwerpen 1990, Kluwer

CHAPTER 5

Effective resolution of collective labour disputes in Germany

Ulrich Zachert

1 State law, collective agreements, work agreements

As in many European Union countries,[1] with the exception of Anglo-Saxon cultures, strong legislation has been developed in virtually all areas of German labour and social welfare law. It ranges from the legal regulation of working hours to holiday entitlements, continuation of pay in cases of illness, protection against unfair dismissal. In addition, it covers groups especially in need of protection, such as young people and the severely disabled. In contrast to Spain and France, to cite two examples, there is no uniform German labour code.[2] Likewise, in contrast to many neighbouring countries, the German legislator has not yet passed a minimum wage law. The unions are (still) strong enough to settle this central labour relations issue independently through a collective agreement.[3]

Collective agreements are typically concluded with a normative, that is automatic and mandatory effect, following § 4 *Tarifvertragsgesetz* (*TVG*) (Act on Collective Agreements) at the regional level. The number of newly negotiated or modified collective agreements each year is consistently somewhere between 6000-7000. There are more than 60.000 *Flächentarifverträge* (regional or area collective agreements) and approximately 27.000 *Firmentarifverträge* (single-company collective agreements) currently in effect.[4]

In accordance with § 3 par. 1 *TVG*, collective agreements are only binding when both parties are members of their respective organizations, that is unions and employers associations. The level of trade union membership is about 25%. However, in practice, collective agreements apply to approximately 70% of all employees. Especially important here, in addition to the declaration of generally applicability (*erga omnes* applicability) according to § 5 *TVG*, is the fact that individual employment contracts overwhelmingly refer to the relevant collective bargaining contract, and therefore their standards are reflected in the content of individual legal relationships.

Unlike the legal systems of many of our neighbouring European countries, the general view is that collective agreements are bound by an (relative) obligation to keep peace. During the term of the collective bargaining contract, the parties to the agreement refrain from engaging in industrial actions and must prevent their members from engaging in industrial actions or from bringing about a deterioration of working conditions.[5]

1 See also F. Valdés Dal-Ré (2003), especially for Germany the report of Zachert 171 with further information and different main emphasis.

2 For the time being the last attempt of the work group 'Uniformity in German Labour Law', Report D to 59, German Law Congress (1992).

3 However in the construction industry a minimum wage applies according to the *Entsendegesetz* (Employment Delegate Law) of 1996; the Law on the Establishment of Minimum Work Conditions of 1952 has not been applied yet.

4 Annual statistics of the Federal Ministry of (Economics and) Labour, lastly 2004.

5 Paradigmatic BAG 21. 12. 1982, *AP* No. 76 to Article 9 GG *Arbeitskampf*.

In addition to the traditional issues of wages and work hours, settlements on job security and qualifications play an important role. The relationship between state and collective bargaining law can be characterized in the following way: the law establishes a minimum level of protection for labour that is improved by collective agreements in many areas.

Work agreements are likewise collective agreements and, in accordance with § 77 of the *Betriebsverfassungsgesetz* (*BetrVG*) (Works Council Act), are in many ways similar in their effect to collective agreements. The parties, however, are the works council elected by all employees and the employer of the respective company. The main competence of the works councils are the so-called 'matters of social concern' in which they can have an enforceable right to participate in management decisions (§ 87 *BetrVG*). Collective agreements take precedence over work agreements (§ 77 par. 3, and § 87 par. 1 *BetrVG*).

2 Conflict resolution

To understand conflict resolution, collective and shop agreements must be rigorously differentiated. The means for breaking the silence between unions and employers associations (or one single employer) to reach a collective agreement are industrial actions, such as strikes and limited lock outs. The prevailing view is that, functionally, industrial actions very clearly refer to the right to free collective bargaining, and the promoter of a strike is not the individual employee but the union.[6] Industrial action is assumed to be an institution of the right to free collective bargaining, as otherwise neither the realization nor the appropriateness of collective bargaining agreements could be guaranteed.[7]

Court decisions have given the parties to collective bargaining a special responsibility to reach conciliation agreements containing provisions that resolve clashes of interests.[8]

In contrast, company internal work agreements may not be pushed trough by industrial actions. § 74, par. 2 *BetrVG* expressively forbids the parties to a work agreement from engaging in industrial actions. In this case, conflicts are resolved by the so-called *Einigungsstelle* (conciliation committee/board) according to § 76 *BetrVG* what can be described as an 'institutional internal conciliation proceeding'.

6 Description and critique Zachert (2001) *AuR* 401.

7 BAG 10. 6. 1980, *AP* No. 64 to Article 9 GG *Arbeitskampf*; in this respect nothing is said about lock outs.

8 BAG *Großer Senat*, 21. 4. 1971, *AP* No. 43 to Article 9 GG *Arbeitskampf*.

3 The role of the state and the actors in collective bargaining conflicts

3.1 Historical background

The role of the state in bringing about and promoting conciliation in German labour law has been marked by great restraint. Of more practical importance are the already mentioned collective bargaining conciliation agreements. These are proceedings in which the parties themselves reach an agreement. In contrast, the offer of (voluntary) state conciliation, which is also available, is only taken advantage of to a limited extent.

There are mainly two reasons to explain the clear preference for non-governmental conciliation proceedings.

The first reason is that Germany has comparatively well established labour courts which also have jurisdiction over collective labour law. This is in stark contrast to the English system of conflict resolution with its Advisory Conciliation and Arbitration Service (Acas), available to the parties in addition to the labour courts.[9]

The second reason is based in history. Starting in 1923, during the Weimar Republic, there was compulsory state conciliation.[10] This led to the unions losing some of their autonomy and the breakdown of the labour law structure,[11] which since 1918 had been extensively based on the concept of collective bargaining autonomy as developed by Hugo Sinzheimer, that is to say agreement on collective bargaining contracts without state intervention.[12] Therefore, to this day in Germany there are provisions that only require the state's assistance in making voluntary conciliation available. In fact, there was agreement after the Second World War that the responsibility for determining procedural rules for conciliation of collective bargaining conflicts would lie principally with the collective bargaining parties themselves.[13] State conciliation was to be available only on a voluntary basis and merely as an alternative.[14]

---

9 Kahn-Freund (1979) 101; Binker/Reber (2001) *AuR* 163; Towers/Brown (2000); comprehensive legally comparative references, see Gamillscheg (1997) 1003.

10 In more detail, Raupach (1964) 54; Kocher (2000) *DLRI* 463.

11 Cf. Kahn-Freund (1966) 211.

12 On the importance of Sinzheimer, see Zachert (2001) *RdA* 104.

13 Nautz (1985) 147.

14 Institutional conciliation proceedings for groups of persons who cannot push through collective agreements such as home workers (§ 18 following Home Workers Act) or similar groups such as authors.

3.2 The legal basis

3.2.1 General overview

Conciliation proceedings in collective bargaining conflicts are overwhelmingly based on agreements between the collective bargaining parties that legally befit the character of collective agreements with obligatory effects.[15] They are very different in their arrangement and scope. In fact, model conciliation agreements were drafted in the 1950s between the German Trade Union Federation and the National Union of Employers' Associations. However, for various reasons, these did not prove effective and are therefore no longer of great importance today.[16]

The right to free collective bargaining guaranteed by the constitution (Article 9, par. 3 *Grundgesetz* (*GG*)) is the legal justification of conciliation by virtue of the agreement between the parties. Since conciliation procedures agreed upon by the parties result from the right to free collective bargaining, they have priority over state conciliation.[17]

State conciliation in collective bargaining conflicts has their legal basis in a law from the period of occupation immediately after the Second World War, and before the foundation of the Federal Republic of Germany. The so-called Control Council Act no. 35 of 1946 remains in effect as a federal law today. It stipulates that the federal employment authorities are to appoint experts from their staff who have the task of advising employers and their organizations, the parties to collective bargaining, and of acting as intermediary between them.[18] Most German *Länder* (Federal States) have passed special implementation ordinances for these so-called 'state conciliators.'[19]

'Conciliation' by the company internal conciliation committee/board is legally based on § 76 and following the Works Council Act, which determines the basic terms of procedure.

3.2.2 The public sector

In 2005 there were approximately 2.5 million employees in the public sector and 1.7 million public officials. Conciliation proceedings in collective bargaining conflicts are also common for employees in the public sector, however not for *Beamte* (public officials).

Public officials enjoy the right to free association, Article 9, par. 3 *GG* and § 91 of the *Bundesbeamtengesetz* (Federal Civil Service Act), but collective agree-

15 Kempen/Zachert (2006), § 1 Rn. 630 following with documentation.

16 In more detail, Behning (1994) 103; Knevels (1988) *ZTR* 408.

17 Generally held opinion, *e.g.* Gamillscheg (1997) 1306.

18 Lembke (2000) *RdA* 223.

19 In more detail, Löwisch (1997) 477, Rn. 57 following.

ments do not apply to them. Their pay and other employment terms are determined by law, § 2 *Bundesbesoldungsgesetz* (Federal Pay Act for Public Officials).

In addition to that, § 4 of the *Bundespersonalvertretungsgesetz* (Federal Public Employees' Representation Act) and accordingly the respective Federal State Employees' Representation Acts, apply to public officials so that internal conciliation proceedings by conciliation committees in civil service administration also cover public officials. In so far the co-determination rights of the *Personalrat* (staff council) are limited according to § 76 of the *Bundespersonalvertretungsgesetz*.

4 Typology of conflict resolution

German law, just as in other countries, makes a distinction between conciliation, mediation, and arbitration.[20] However, the practical emphasis is clearly on conciliation and the term mediation (mediator) first entered into German legal terminology from the Anglo-American experience.

Conciliation means the ending of a conflict (over interests) by a third party who renders a conciliation judgement after the presentation of the facts and circumstances by the parties. The procedural rules, the authority of the conciliator and the effect of the conciliation judgement are at the discretion of the parties.

This applies, above all, to conciliation in collective bargaining conflicts, agreed upon between the parties. It is also up to them, unions and employers associations or a single employer, to finance the 'body'. But it is a conciliation *ad hoc*, that generally means that the conciliation body ceases to exist if the conflict has been solved.

For the few cases of state conciliation proceedings there is a professional chairman, the so-called 'regional conciliator', who must have sufficient expertise in matters of production, employment and labour relations. This is mostly an employee in the public sector. This person is played by the public authorities.

For company internal conciliation by the conciliation committee/board, as already indicated, the provisions of § 76, par. 2 and 3 of the Works Council Act make certain procedural rules compulsory, and § 77, par. 1 Works Council Act adds a compulsory effect to the ruling of the conciliation committee in matters of co-determination. The costs of the internal conciliation committee/board are borne by the employer, § 76 a Works Council Act. Also this type of conciliation is an *ad hoc* proceeding.

Mediation is a voluntary proceeding for which there is still no legal regulation in Germany. Mediation involves the balancing of interests. The parties determine the course of the proceedings. The mediator has no power to take

[20] On concepts and the respective differences, see overview in: Albrecht (2001) 27.

decisions. If the conflict is resolved, the mediation agreement normally has the effect of a private law contract.

Arbitration means that a third party, the arbitrator has the power to decide, and to render a decision through an arbitral award. The court of arbitration primarily decides legal disputes, which means conflicts that involve the determination or application of state legal provisions. In labour law, arbitration is considerably restricted. Under § 101 *Arbeitsgerichtsgesetz* (Labour Courts Act), only the parties to the collective bargaining conflict can call in the courts of arbitration and then to a limited extent. The reason for this is the concern that protection of the employee in arbitration could be viewed in labour law as insufficient.[21]

5 Practical importance, empirical data on conflict resolution

There is no precise information on how many agreed conciliation proceedings in collective bargaining conflicts are actually conducted per year or in any other reference period. However, it can be assumed that conciliation agreements have been reached by parties to collective bargaining contracts in virtually all of the big industries of the private economy and in the civil service. This means that there are collective agreements in effect for about two thirds of employees in which the parties have concluded agreements for conciliation.[22] Of course, this does not necessarily mean that they have been applied in collective bargaining conflicts. This does, however, mean that there is no single year in which a collective bargaining contract is not reached through an agreed conciliation proceeding. This seems reasonable to suppose because, quantitatively, the right to free collective bargaining continues to be of great importance. Every year, as already mentioned, about 6000-7000 collective agreements are renewed or newly concluded.

By contrast, state conciliation proceedings in collective bargaining conflicts are used only to a very limited extent. From 1988 to 1995, only 50 conciliation proceedings were conducted by the so-called ‘regional conciliators’ of the different Federal States.[23]

According to facts from a regular survey, conducted over a two-year period, there were internal conciliation committee proceedings in about 16% of all companies (with works councils) in the period of 1999-2000.[24] There are no

[21] In more detail, Langer (1994), 465.

[22] Information from the Federal Ministry of Labour from September 2005; this coincides with the figures of Gamillscheg (1997) 1036.

[23] Löwisch (1997) 458, Rn. 5; in: Berlin/Brandenburg, according to information of June 2000 from the regional conciliator, Dr. Horst Weigand, there are about 10 proceedings per year for individual companies or smaller industries.

[24] Dorsch-Schweizer/Schulten, (2001) *WSI Mitt.* 113.

figures available on mediation in collective labour law, since this form of out-of-court conciliation of disputes (still) does not exist in German labour law.[25]

Courts of arbitration, as already explained, are only active in labour law under very limited conditions. Their importance, quantitatively, is extraordinarily limited in comparison to labour court conflict resolution in general. Statistics in this respect are apparently not kept.

6 Critical assessment

6.1 Collective bargaining conciliation arranged by agreement

Collective bargaining conciliation in German labour law has two functions.[26] One important objective is to avoid industrial actions or to assist to bring them to an end. Beyond that, another purpose in collective conflicts is to find a compromise of interests.[27] For an understanding of the legal situation in Germany, it is important to emphasize that unlike most other countries, according to general interpretation, an obligation to keep the peace is inherent to the collective agreement. From this, it follows that this obligation may be extended or even limited, depending on how the conciliation proceedings are arranged.

In the collective bargaining practices, there are industries that rely heavily on the conciliation proceeding itself to resolve collective bargaining conflicts. The chemical industry is paradigmatic in this with an automatic call for conciliation, equal representation in the composition of the conciliation commission, no impartial chairman, a majority decision, and an obligation to keep the peace that ends only when it has been decided that the conciliation proceedings have broken down.

In other industries, the conciliation proceedings are arranged in such a way that the resolution of the conflict is maintained at the forefront through the collective bargaining negotiations themselves including industrial actions (strikes). An example of this is the metal industry, which remains a pioneer in pushing through wage demands. In the metal industry there is no obligation to accept conciliation in the sense of an automatic conciliation. Of the two chairmen, the one with the power to vote is determined by lot, and the obligation to keep the peace ends, independently of the conciliation proceedings, four weeks after expiration of the (former) collective bargaining agreement.

With this differentiation, collective bargaining conciliation, agreed by the respective parties, is accepted in German labour law. This applies to the future

25 For sceptical perspectives on individual law and the Works Council Act, see Albrecht (2001) 122.

26 Külp (1972) 9, 112.

27 See *e.g.* Gamillscheg (1997) 1299.

as well. The principle of having the collective bargaining parties themselves agree on the conciliation arrangements facilitates open and flexible adaptation to new requirements and evolutions.

6.2 Internal conciliation through a conciliation committee or board

Company internal conciliation through a conciliation committee/board has a distinct purpose. In this case, it involves the removal of obstacles that arise in conflicts over matters of co-determination rights in the company. Despite criticism of particulars, such as the cost level, the conciliation committee/board is overwhelmingly seen as an organ that is in a position to bring about a relatively swift resolution to internal conflicts specific to the conditions at the respective company.[28] There are no perceivable tendencies in legal policy that might bring changes in the near future to this fundamentally positive assessment and to the practical importance of the conciliation committee/board.

6.3 Mediation and arbitration

Mediation, which has as yet no great importance in German labour law, will probably receive it, above all because of its wide-open possibilities for the future. The limits arise from the fact that there is currently no room for mediation where other proceedings, such as those of internal conciliation committees/boards, lead to satisfactory solutions. In individual labour law, for which the labour courts are available to resolve conflicts, the limits of this kind of conflict resolution are based on the fact that there is generally an imbalance of power to the prejudice of the employee. So he might be in better hands with the labour courts, which are well experienced in social conflicts and decide the case on the whole quite rapidly and efficiently. With these limitations, the future of mediation could be seen as having a complementary function for other already existing conciliation proceedings.[29]

Presumably because of the very limited scope of jurisdiction that arbitration is accorded in German labour law, there is no controversy about its importance. It is accepted in the given framework.

[28] *E.g.* the assessment by Kocher (2000) *DLRI* 463, 498 with references.

[29] Cf. Albrecht (2001) 122.

7 European perspectives

The unbroken dynamic in the growth of European companies, and the number of conflicts of transnational dimension linked with it,[30] as well as the extension of participation rights,[31] are all indications that, in the case of dissent, suitable opportunities for solutions are available or can be provided when they are absent. The five framework agreements which, in accordance with Article 139 EC, have been converted into directives are certainly not more than a first step.

Against the backdrop of the traditional structures for conflict resolution in German labour law, conciliation proceedings at the European level will have a chance of being accepted by labour and management if they are strictly voluntary and do not replace the existing conflict resolution but complement it. In addition, access to the courts should not be excluded or cut back.

Under these conditions, there should also be no serious objections to an 'institutional offer' of conciliation experts. Panels of this kind, familiar to other legal systems (like Great Britain and Spain), are alien to German labour law. However, perhaps the complexity of transnational conflicts, language difficulties, as well as legal and cultural peculiarities of the respective countries speaks for the establishment of an 'institutional conciliation body' at the European level.

30 See the Renault-Vilvoorde conflict, Arbeitsrechtsbank van Brussel (Brussels Labour Court) 3. 4. 1997 (1997) AuR 366; further Caron/Weinert (2005) *Transfer* 261.

31 Directive 2002/14/EC of 11. March 2002 establishing a general framework for informing and consulting employees in the European Community.

Bibliography

ALBRECHT (2001)
B. Albrecht, *Mediation im Arbeitsrecht* (Frankfurt am Main 2001) Peter Lang

BEHNING (1994)
B. Behning, *Die Schlichtung der kollektiven Arbeitsverfassung der Bundesrepublik Deutschland* (Frankfurt am Main 1994) Peter Lang

BINKERT/REBER (2001)
G. Binkert/D. Reber, Gegenwartsprobleme der französischen und britischen Arbeitsgerichtsbarkeit (2001) *AuR* 163-166

CARON/WEINERT (2005)
Ch. Caron/R. Weinert, The EMF European Company Policy: the GME Restructuring and Framwork Agreement (2005) *Transfer* 260-267

DORSCH-SCHWEIZER/SCHULTEN (2001)
M. Dorsch-Schweizer/ Th. Schulten, Betriebs- und Personalräte zwischen Belegschaft, Arbeitgeber und Gewerkschaft (2001) *WSI Mitt.* 113-123

FEDERAL MINISTERY OF ECONOMICS AND LABOUR (2004)
Federal Ministery of Economics and Labour, *Tarifvertragliche Arbeitsbedingungen im Jahr 2004*) (Bonn 2004) own printing

GAMILLSCHEG (1997)
F. Gamillscheg, *Kollektives Arbeitsrecht* (München 1997) Beck

KAHN-FREUND (1979)
O. Kahn-Freund, *Arbeit und Recht* (Köln 1979) Bund-Verlag

KAHN-FREUND (1966)
O. Kahn-Freund, Der Funktionswandel des Arbeitskampfrechts 211-246, in: Th. Ramm editor, *Arbeitsrecht und Politik* (Neuwied 1966 Luchterhand

KEMPEN/ZACHERT (2006)
O.E. Kempen/U. Zachert, *Tarifvertragsgesetz* 4. edition (Frankfurt am Main 2006) Bund-Verlag

KNEVELS (1988)
P. Knevels, Das Schlichtungsabkommen in der Bundesrepublik (1988) *ZTR* 408-414

KOCHER (2000)
E. Kocher, Arbitrato e conziliatione nel diritto del lavoro tedesco (2000) *DLRI* 463-490.

KÜLP (1972)
B. Külp, *Der Einfluss von Schlichtungsformen auf Verlauf und Ergebnis von Tarif- und Schlichtungsvereinbarungen* (Berlin 1972) Duncker und Humblot

LANGER (1994)
K.A. Langer, Schiedsgerichte in Arbeitssachen 465-482 *Festschrift für den Deutschen Arbeitsgerichtsverband* (Neuwied etc. 1994) Luchterhand

LEMBKE (2000)
M. Lembke, Staatliche Schlichtung in Arbeitsstreitigkeiten nach dem Kontrollratsgesetz (2000) *RdA* 223-235
LÖWISCH (1997)
M. Löwisch, *Arbeitskampf und Schlichtungsrecht* (Heidelberg 1997) Forkel-Verlag
NAUTZ (1985)
J.P. Nautz, *Die Durchsetzung der Tarifautonomie in Westdeutschland* (Frankfurt am Main etc. 1985) Peter Lang
RAUPACH (1964)
H. Raupach, *Die Schlichtung von kollektiven Arbeitsstreitigkeiten und ihre Probleme unter besonderer Berücksichtigung der deutschen Entwicklung* (Berlin 1964) Duncker und Humblot
TOWERS/BROWN (2000)
B. Towers/W. Brown, *Employment Relations in Britain: 25 years of the Adver sory Conciliation and Arbitration Service* (Oxford 2000) Blackwell Publishers
VALDÉS DAL-RÉ (2003)
F. Valdés Dal-Ré, *Labour Conciliation, Mediation and Arbitration in European Union Countries* (Madrid 2003) Ministerio de Trabajo y Asuntos Sociales, also as a spanish edition
ZACHERT (2001)
U. Zachert, Hugo Sinzheimer, praktischer Wissenschaftler und Pionier des modernen Arbeitsrechts (2001) *RdA* 104-109
ZACHERT (2001)
U. Zachert, Wilder Streik noch zeitgemäß? (2001) *AuR* 401-405
ZACHERT (2003)
U. Zachert, Labour Conciliation, Mediation and Arbitration in Germany 171-194, in: F. Valdés Dal-Ré editor, *Labour Conciliation, Mediation and Arbitration in European Countries* (Madrid 2003) Ministerio de Trabajo y Asuntos Sociales

CHAPTER 6

The UK perspective on the provision of alternative dispute resolution processes

Terry Lippiatt

This chapter covers the establishment and functions of the UK's Advisory Conciliation and Arbitration Service (Acas) and also gives an overview of collective bargaining arrangements in the United Kingdom with particular regards to current trends in employment relations and dispute resolution. It also details evaluative research on the benefits of third party interventions.

1 The origins of Acas

In the UK the concept of third party assistance to resolve collective disputes goes back over one hundred years to the Conciliation Act of 1896. The mediation and arbitration function was traditionally carried out by the state, via government departments like the Board of Trade or Ministry of Labour until the early 1970's when, following the 'Donovan Commission' report into the state of British industrial relations and a fairly unpopular, government imposed, period of prices and income control, the trade unions and employer's organizations proposed that an independent body be set up to provide impartial alternative dispute resolution processes. This explains why the Social Partners have been supportive of Acas over its 30 years of existence and probably why Acas was left unscathed during the years when the British Conservative Party was engaged in major trade union reform.

2 Acas duties and functions

The Advisory Conciliation and Arbitration Service (Acas) was set up as a statutory body on 1 January 1976. Its functions and duties are:

- to advise employers, workers, unions and businesses on employment relations and employment policy matters. The main delivery arm is a telephone helpline which deals with almost 1 million enquiries per year;
- to prepare codes of practice relating to good employment standards, currently 3 in number – Discipline and Grievance, Time Off for Trade Union Activities and Disclosure of Information for Collective Bargaining Purposes;
- to designate staff as conciliation officers to provide assistance in complaints made by individuals under legislation on employment rights. Around 300 Acas officers perform this function dealing with about 85,000 cases per year. Although Acas has a statutory duty to conciliate and attempt to settle cases, use of Acas conciliation by the disputing parties is still voluntary;
- to conciliate/mediate in collective employment disputes. Around 50 full time staff are employed in this activity dealing with on average, 1,200 cases per year;
- to arrange independent directive mediation and arbitration. A panel

of about 100 independent persons is maintained. These independent persons are mainly arbitrators but some also have mediation skills. They are assigned and paid on a case by case basis. They arbitrate trade disputes or conduct hearings where formal, but non-binding, mediation with recommendations is required by the parties;
- to maintain a panel of Independent Experts to be made available to the Employment Tribunal Service in Equal Pay claims (Under Equal Pay Amendment Regulations 1983 (SI 1983 1794);
- to provide a Secretariat for the Police Arbitration Tribunal.

Under the Trade Union and Labour Relations (Consolidation) Act 1992 sections 254-265 Acas is required to provide both the Certification Officer (CO) and the Central Arbitration Committee (CAC) with staff. The CO is responsible for the registration and integrity of independent trades unions and the CAC is the court which deals with complaints regarding trade union recognition, information and consultation arrangements and failure to disclose information for collective bargaining.

The Service is funded by the UK government through its Department of Trade and Industry (DTI) on a running cost basis. The cost of the Service is currently around € 70 million per year.

Acas has an overarching duty of promoting the improvement of employment relations in the UK and this service is available to both the private and public sector. The Service also has a general duty to promote equality, to promote good relations between different racial groups and to eliminate discrimination.

In the UK government's opinion, these facilities meet the requirement of Article 6 of the European Social Charter.

3 Collective bargaining in the UK

Historically, collective bargaining in the UK is typified by the 'voluntary' approach and although many sectors use Acas facilities, they are not required by law to turn to Acas. Even at the arbitration stage Acas awards are not legally binding. But it is true that over many years the morally binding obligation has been upheld by the social partners and is still the preferred method of resolving collective disputes. This 'voluntary' approach also applies to collective agreements, which, with few exceptions, are morally rather than legally binding documents. In the UK recourse to the law to enforce or interpret collective agreements is a rare event.

In practice referral of disputes to Acas forms part of many collective agreements. Acas has become a well known and well regarded institution over the years and, even where no formal agreement exists, there is nothing to stop the parties seeking Acas assistance either jointly or unilaterally. Acas also offers its services on its own initiative when it becomes aware of a dispute.

Turning to the delivery of Acas services in the public and private sectors the distinguishing features which have grown up over the past 20 years are:

- trade union density in the private sector has greatly decreased whilst it has remained high in the public sector;
- national bargaining has virtually disappeared in the private sector, but is still significant in the public sector;
- the development of a partnership relationship in both sectors has had an effect on attitudes to employment related disputes.

The key difference in levels of strike activity in the UK is that strike action is almost entirely confined to the public sector. In recent times this has involved the fire service employees over pay, central government employees over pensions and local government workers over 'single status' and equal pay.

Although this has led for many calls for a ban on strike action in public services this has not generally won government backing. However strike action is outlawed in the armed forces, the police and prison service.

In the UK there are a number of restrictions on the right to strike which apply to all sectors. Majority approval must be given in a strike ballot and the ballot must be conducted by an independent third party. Notice of strike action and details of which workers intend to strike must be given. Strike action must begin within four weeks of the ballot result.

Legislation protects employees in two ways. Firstly, individuals cannot be identified and secondly, no worker can be dismissed unless they have been on continuous strike, at the moment for eight weeks, but this is soon to be amended to 12 weeks.

The institutionalization of strike action has lead to a tendency in both the private and public sectors to use the ballot result as a pressure point to get the employer to return to the negotiating table in a more meaningful frame of mind. If the parties are making progress the four week strike notification can be extended to allow a further four weeks talks to take place.

4 Acas' unique perspective and evaluative research

If Acas is involved in any of its dispute resolution modes, the service always looks for underlying problems and promotes its advisory service to try to persuade the parties to seek better ways of working together such as partnership or improved procedures.

As a general rule mediators and arbitrators are trained to concentrate on the substance of the dispute across all sectors. In the past two to three years the UK Government and the public sector unions have agreed far reaching arrangements to deal with the outsourcing of government contracts and the protection of workers pay and conditions in such circumstance.

Acas research has shown that in 2004 around 90% of collective conciliations have a successful outcome.[1] Independent research in 2002 found that 77% of the parties surveyed said that the agreement finally reached was acceptable and 82% said that it offered practical outcomes to the dispute. Overall 88% of customers said they were satisfied with the service and 92% said that, following their experience of conciliation in the dispute they would use Acas services in the future.

Acas customers also reported long-term improvements through collective conciliation. These included improvements in employee morale (22%), profitability (5%), competitiveness (7%), performance (11%) and workplace practices (25%). There were also improvements in the co-operation between the sides (36%), communication between sides (39%), understanding of the other side's position (39%) and working closer together (30%).

'Partnership' is anything from a high-trust industrial relations agenda with an explicit objective of combining business advantage with gains for employees in terms of job security and improvements in their working lives, to a low key but joint approach to sorting things out. This joint approach is at the heart of Acas workplace improvement projects, their advisory work. The economic benefits of what is described as partnership have been well documented.

For example, a survey by Industrial Relations Services found that some six in ten of organizations which had adopted partnership arrangements identified bottom line improvements which they attributed specifically to their employee relations policies. Over half of these identified the benefits in financial terms. SmithKline Beecham said it had saved £7.2 million from implementing business process engineering, Blue Circle Cement had saved £2 million a year on delivery fleet operating costs, and Dunlop GRG mentioned increased sales and profit per employee. Airedale NHS Trust said that their bottom line improvements were too numerous to describe, but included increased throughput, quality and care improvement and efficiency gains. Remploy achieved £1 million of increased throughput from absence reduction while Littlewoods Home Shopping group said there were higher sales and less complaints. Many of the organizations that could not identify bottom line benefits believed that there were such benefits but they could not yet be quantified.[2]

The Department of Trade and Industry 'Partnership at Work Fund' funded up to 50% of the cost of projects designed to increase effective consultation, employee voice and reciprocity between management and employees. The outcomes of the exercise were formally evaluated by the DTI.[3] The evaluation found that the process of improving relations between management and unions:

- facilitated change – a small non-union engineering company, for example, was able to implement changes in holiday times and entitlements, intro-

1 Acas, *Coming to the table*, Acas: London 2004.

2 Industrial Relations Services, *Partnership at work: a survey*, IRS Employment Trends, 1997, 645.

3 M. Terry and J. Smith, Evaluation of Partnership at Work Fund, in: *Employment Relations Research Series*, No. 17, 2003.

duce outsourcing and make some redundancies without dispute;
- reduced formal disputes/grievances/discipline cases – one privatized utility claimed that contentious issues were approached more constructively, another was able to resolve a dispute painlessly and a third achieved cost savings because better working relationship between stewards and managers resolved issues at local level;
- improved retention – a large food conglomerate saw a decrease in labour turnover from 20% to 10%, and an engineering company from 30% to 22%;
- reduced absence – a private sector organization said that absence fell from 4.8% to 2% as a result of a consultation process which was able to establish a fair policy and an understanding of the policy;
- improved the bottom line – a food and drink company had saved £1.4 million over two years as a result of a waste-reduction programme;
- enabled private companies to gain public contracts. One said that it had been able to win a new housing benefits contract as a result of its partnership work and another said that effective working relationships between unions and employees, including rapid response to change and a decline in disciplinary cases enabled it to compete more effectively and win contracts.

Acas research in 2004 and 2002 found that trust improved as a result of Acas advisory work to improve employee relations.[4] Marked improvements in employee satisfaction followed on from an Acas partnership-building exercise in a government body while in a manufacturing firm managers described a direct and positive link between the outcomes of an Acas facilitated change programme and improvements in company performance. These included improvements in machine efficiencies, a halving of absence levels and an increase in productivity of over 20%.

Acas has also recently evaluated its new pilot mediation service. In addition to resolving the dispute or improving the situation a wide range of benefits were reported by both employers and employees. For instance, employers reported that they had gained more confidence in their ability to manage conflict and to use their own internal workplace procedures. Employers also reported enormous savings in time and money as mediation led to quicker resolutions than internal discipline and grievance procedures and also reduced the costs of seeking external advice from employer associations and accountants. The majority of employers were also of the opinion that the mediation had helped to prevent employment tribunal applications.[5]

---

4 Acas, *Coming to the table*, Acas: London 2004.

5 Acas, *Evaluation of the Acas Pilot of Mediation, Appeals and Employment Law Visit Services to Small Firms*, Acas: London 2005.

Academics have been searching for many years to identify the links between ways of managing people and organizational performance. And while many were able to show an association between policies and performance outcomes, it was often hard to explain when, why and how this association existed and to identify the interconnections. This has become known as the 'black box problem'. A three-year study commissioned by the Chartered Institute of Personnel and Development found a number of clear linkages: employee commitment leads to higher levels of organizational performance, and commitment is greater in organizations with good communications and employee involvement, while a poor climate of employee relations damages employee commitment.[6]

Interestingly, the HR directors of the organizations being studied believed that profit and shareholder value are lag indicators of historical interest only and that the direct connection between people management and ultimate measure is too stretched or distant with too many other variables influencing profit. But three types of measures are used: labour market indicators such as labour turnover, retention, absence and accidents; employee satisfaction measures, which are increasingly correlated with customer satisfaction survey results and operational measures such as down time, scrap rates or on-time deliveries.

Hay Management Consultants has an engaged performance™ model, a concept designed to gain engagement and commitment to organizational success. Hay says that from its experience, satisfied employees are 30% less likely to leave the organization, and that there is a demonstrable link between engagement and high levels of organizational performance. It also says that employees are now more knowledgeable and more cynical about employer behaviour, as well as being more confident and assertive, so employers now need greater skills to get the best out of their workforce.

Good employee relations are a prerequisite for the changes in working practices that are needed to enable UK companies to compete in a global market place and the employee motivation and commitment, which are increasingly being seen as critical to organizational performance. If employees do not trust their employer, they will neither give of their best nor agree to change.

In 2000 the Chancellor of the Exchequer asked the Confederation of British Industry (CBI) and the Trade Union Congress (TUC) to work together to address the challenge of raising productivity in the UK. Their joint report, issued in 2001, stated that closing the productivity gap required the wider adoption of best practice throughout the economy. And in 2003 the DTI strategy – Prosperity for all – was announced: the analysis, concluded that "[...] new forms of work organisation, effective management leadership, a culture that encourages innovation, employee involvement and development tailored to organisational needs are all necessary conditions for adaptable, high performance workplaces."

---

[6] J. Purcell, *The HRM-performance link: why, how and when does people management impact on organisational performance?*, James Lovett Memorial Lecture, University of Limerick 2004.

A number of studies have shown that high-performance workplace practices can raise employee commitment and morale and reduce absenteeism and staff turnover, which leads to higher productivity.[7]

The characteristics of a high-performance workplace are:

- modern employee management practices that develop workforce skills and use them flexibly within the workplace;
- good communications that work both upwards and downwards and enable employee involvement;
- a spirit of trust and mutual commitment to common goals between employers and employees.

Team working, joint problem solving, quality circles, strong appraisal systems, team briefings and effective structures for information and consultation are examples of these practices.

First findings from the 2004 Workplace Employment Relations Survey suggest that only 16% of workplaces employing 28% of employees have a large number of these practices in place, up from 13% in 1998. Adding a requirement to operate problem-solving groups reduces the incidence to 6% of workplaces employing 15% of employees. There is no single factor blocking the take up, according to WERS 2004, although attitudes to change, insufficient time, a lack of understanding of the benefits and a lack of workforce or management skills all play a part.

The large proportion of UK workplaces not using the high-performance working practices required in a global economy suggests an urgent need for government encouragement and support, as presently offered by Acas.

At the present time there are two further significant factors in the UK which are worthy of note. Firstly there is an ongoing debate about the need to promote the whole range of alternative dispute resolution strategies in order to prevent society becoming 'litigation minded' in the way we regard much of the pursuance of 'damages' and ambulance chasing in the USA. Recently our 'Better Regulation Task Force' warned the government of the need to counter this by providing alternatives such as mediation.

Secondly in the field of collective dispute resolution the growing emphasis is away from the formal processes of mediation and arbitration and a move towards 'assisted negotiation'. This is a very specific application of mediation and has its immediate origin in the report of the independent 2004 Local Government Pay Commission. It is primarily targeted, although not exclusively,

---

7 M.E. Porter and C.H.M. Ketels, *UK competitiveness: moving to the next stage*, DTI Economics Paper, No. 3, 2003; D. Bosworth, *Empirical evidence of management skills in the UK*, Skills Task Force Research Paper 18, 2000; M.G. Patterson, M.A. West, R. Lawthorn and S. Nickell, The impact of people management practices on business performance, IPD issues, in: *People Management*, No. 22, 1997.

at public services. It involves a particular form of third party intervention, which the Commission labelled 'assisted bargaining'. Acas collective conciliation has traditionally been focused at the point in negotiations where parties have exhausted their disputes procedures and reached a stalemate. Whilst we will continue to meet this demand, we will also offer conciliation at an earlier stage, in line with the recommendations of the Commission, before any formal 'failure to agree' in the traditional sense is registered. This will involve conciliation or mediation to help unblock stalled negotiations and/or assist the parties to arrive at their own outcome.

This approach is particularly relevant to the new partnership arrangements Acas is trying to foster in the public sector. Acas old policy was only to intervene 'once all domestic procedures have been exhausted'. Although this practice ensures that the parties make their own efforts to resolve differences before calling in a third party, many commentators note that the traditional Alternative Dispute Resolution (ADR) processes of mediation and arbitration start off in situations where both sides have rehearsed their arguments many times and invariably are entrenched in their positions. Earlier intervention, before a final breakdown, could assist and support negotiators on both sides. One of the facts of business life is that negotiating a deal is a skilful process where even the 'old hands' sometimes come unstuck. Equally newcomers to the negotiating arena often lack skill and experience and become trapped in 'deadlocks', sometimes because of a particular style or behaviour .

Most public services involve national negotiations, which makes it possible to establish basic frameworks of terms and conditions that serve the interests of both employers and trade unions. National negotiations have a downside, though, which is that any breakdown means that the coverage of any dispute is likely to be exceptionally wide. Moreover, many public services involve life and death activities and any disruption can have fatal consequences as well as massively inconveniencing large numbers of members of the public. Experience in this and other countries suggests that banning industrial action rarely has the desired effect and does little, if anything, to resolve the underlying issues. This is above all true of the major change issues that are so dominating relationships in the public services in the UK. Employers and trade unions in public services need to reflect the changing emphasis by modernising the procedures for handling their relationships. The focus needs to be on processes for managing change rather than handling disputes. Like the Local Government Pay Commission, Acas view is that 'assisted negotiation' has a significant role to play as one of these processes.

CHAPTER 7

Conciliation and mediation in collective labour disputes in Finland[1]

Juhani Salonius

1 Legislation

In Finland, when the parties have failed to negotiate a new collective agreement, the dispute must be referred to conciliation and mediation. Detailed regulations on conciliation and mediation procedure are contained in the Labour Disputes Act of 1962.

The collective bargaining procedure between the labour market organizations is not governed by statutory provisions. In the private sector, negotiations and procedures mainly derive from established practice, although the terms of the collective agreements governing notice to terminate agreements may contain stipulations relating to future negotiations, such as terms regarding amendment proposals to be submitted to the other party. The public-sector negotiations and their procedures are subject to more detailed regulation through provisions in the 'principal agreements'.

Anyone intending a work stoppage or extension of a work stoppage due to a labour dispute must give advance notice to the competent conciliator and to the other party at least two weeks before the scheduled start of the stoppage or its extension.

The obligation to give advance notice applies to anyone intending a work stoppage, irrespective of its scale, the branch in question or whether the stoppage is arranged by an organization or, for instance, by an unorganized group of employees. The scope of the obligation to give advance notice, however, has been restricted in several ways. First, the advance notice obligation concerns only work stoppages, such as strikes and lockouts. All other forms of industrial action – such as blockades, mass resignations, mass dismissals, deliberate go-slow campaigns, overtime bans – fall outside the scope of the advance notice.

Secondly, advance notice even on an intended work stoppage has to be given only if the stoppage has arisen because of a labour dispute. The Act does not apply to a dispute concerning a collective agreement and falling under the jurisdiction of the Labour Court or arbitrators. The obligation to give advance notice only applies to 'disputes of interest', the aim of which is a new collective agreement. This also means that 'purely' political work stoppages or sympathetic actions are not covered by this obligation. The central organizations, however, have recommended that a four-day advance notice be used with sympathetic industrial action.

---

1 The text is partly based on a more comprehensive report by Juhani Salonius, published in 'Labour Conciliation, Mediation and Arbitration in European Union Countries', a collation of the reports produced in the context of a research project within the range of programmes supporting the social dialogue in Europe, with Fernando Valdés Dal-Ré as Director, Colección Informes y Estudios; Serie Relationes Laborales, Núm. 53, Madrid 2003.

2 Conciliation

For the purpose of providing mediation in labour disputes between employers and workers or civil servants and with the object of furthering the relations between the same, there shall be permanent positions for two national conciliators. One of the two posts may be left vacant if the duties of conciliation can be handled by a single national conciliator. This is the actual situation at present.

A conciliation board may be appointed for a particular conciliation duty. This kind of a conciliation body, however, has been used only three times during the past 30 years.

The Act on Mediation in Labour Disputes (1962) stipulates the tasks of the conciliators as follows. It shall be the duty of the national conciliators:

1) in co-operation with the labour market organisations, to endeavour to further the relationships between employers and workers or civil servants and their organisations;
2) at the request of the parties, to preside over negotiations for the conclusion of workers' and civil servants' collective agreements;
3) to direct the work of conciliation in labour disputes throughout the country and, more particularly, to take such conciliation measures as are required by disputes affecting the areas of jurisdiction of two or more district conciliators;
4) to act as chiefs to the district conciliators;
5) where necessary, to instruct a district conciliator, if he so agrees, to carry out a particular conciliation duty outside the latter's territorial competence, either independently or as an assistant to the competent national conciliator;
6) where necessary, to make proposals to the Ministry of Labour for the appointment of a temporary conciliator or an *ad hoc* conciliation board;
7) to carry out the other duties entrusted to them by the Council of State.[2]

The national conciliators have an office attached to the Ministry of Labour and the Finnish conciliation organization is completely financed by the state. The National Conciliator and his secretary are fulltime employees, while the district conciliators function on a part-time basis. There are five conciliation districts for settling disputes of interest in both the public and private sectors. The parties can, if they want to, set up voluntary conciliation bodies, but these are seldom used, nor is there any particular legislation on them. Arbitration is used to some extent to solve both interest and legal disputes. Voluntary arbitration is funded by the parties. The yearly costs for conciliation total approximately € 340,000. The expenses incurred by the parties to the dispute shall be borne by the parties themselves.

---

[2] Act on Mediation in Labour Disputes (420/1962).

The conciliation organization of labour disputes in the public and private sector is the same, and the Labour Court is also available for both. In the government and municipal sectors, there is also a National Dispute Impact Assessment Board functioning in situations of industrial conflicts. If the Board has deemed the projected stoppage of work to be of such a nature that it leads the essential functions of society into a serious state of disturbance, the Board should exhort the parties to remit the industrial action partly or totally. In no case shall one take any measure submitted to the consideration of the Board earlier than after two weeks from the originally announced date of commencing or extending the projected work stoppage. The Board regularly also takes a stand on the limits to a strike and on their significance with regard to the functions of society.

The decision of the Board, however, is a recommendation, and the parties observe it at their discretion.

As to legal proceedings concerning working life, the government and the municipal sectors have their own procedural courses of action, but these legality disputes are not dealt with here.

The provisions governing the disqualification of judges apply to the disqualification of conciliators.

2.1 Arrangement of stoppages of work

It shall not be permissible for a stoppage of work to be extended or commenced in connection with a labour dispute unless the office of the national conciliators and the other party to the dispute have been given notice in writing at least two weeks beforehand, with an indication of the causes of the projected stoppage or the extension of the stoppage, the date of its commencement and its scope. The party giving such notice shall not be permitted, without the consent of the other party, to postpone the commencement or extension of the projected action until a later date than is stated in the notice or to restrict such action to a more limited field.

If a labour dispute is intended to give rise to a work stoppage or the extension of the same that is considered, in the light of its scope or the nature of the sector involved, to affect essential functions of society or to prejudice the general interest to a considerable extent, the Ministry of Labour may, at the proposal of the conciliator or the conciliation board involved, and with the object of reserving sufficient time for mediation, prohibit the projected stoppage or its extension or commencement for a maximum of 14 days from the announced date of its commencement.

In the case of a dispute over the terms of employment of civil servants, the Ministry may extend, for special reasons, at the proposal of the conciliator or conciliation board involved its prohibition of the work stoppage for an additional seven days.

The parties shall attend the negotiations appointed by the conciliator, or shall arrange to be represented at such negotiations, and shall supply such information as the conciliator may deem necessary. Either party may make it a condition that the information supplied should not be revealed without its consent to the other party.

In the discharge of his duties the conciliator shall, after making himself thoroughly conversant with the dispute, with the circumstances of importance in forming an opinion thereon and with the demands of the parties, endeavour to induce the parties to determine the precise matters in dispute and to encourage the parties to agree on the terms of settlement.

One must hold it as a premise that special branch-specific questions are posed to the mediator by the parties. It is in the real interest of the parties to bring forth arguments and facts supporting their stand during the mediation.

If a conciliator fails to settle a dispute by negotiation or in any other manner, he may present the parties with a draft settlement, prepared in writing, at the same time recommending them to accept it within a short time limit, to be fixed by him.

The Labour Disputes Act shall not be applied to any dispute over a workers' or civil servants' collective agreement that calls for consideration by the Labour Court or for arbitration in accordance with the terms of the agreement.

The authorities shall be required, if so requested by a conciliator, to give him any assistance he may need for the performance of his legal duties.

Legislation does not include restraints that would limit preventive measures or the consultation of the parties when labour disputes are imminent. Nowadays it is rather common that the parties turn to the mediating organization even before giving notice of a work stoppage. The success of such voluntary processes depends *i.e.* on the negotiation relations between the parties and on their ability to bear responsibility for their decisions.

If the voluntary mediation process does not lead to any result, and notice of a work stoppage is consequently given, the advantage, however, is that the mediation organization has a more comprehensive understanding of the relevant problems already at the beginning of the mediation.

2.2 The subject of conciliation

In collective labour conflicts, conciliation is used only in disputes over interest. The disputes may concern a single company or a whole branch, and the private sector as well as the public sector. The issues in dispute must be restricted to conditions of employment, not, for instance, ownership, investments or business strategy. In the public sector, where strikes have been permitted since 1970, but all other forms of industrial action except work stoppages are forbidden, the strike has to be connected with collective agreement issues. In other words, those employed by the government and in the municipal sector have a more limited right to industrial action than employees in the private sector. It is not possible to conclude collective agreements on, for instance, the arrangements of the official machinery, the duties of the authorities or internal division of work, the conditions of the eligibility for public offices, pensions and corresponding matters. Therefore these matters may not be promoted by means of industrial action either.

The industrial peace obligation is similar both in the public and private sectors while the collective agreements are valid. In the public sector, the right to strike is very comprehensive. As a rule, only employees functioning as representatives of the employer have no right to resort to industrial action. In addition, in the government sector the judges of the supreme courts and the whole personnel of the Office of the President of the Republic may not take part in industrial action.

Civil servants' unions are not permitted to engage in sympathy strikes.

In Finland, the system of labour relations is based mainly on nationwide collective agreements. These comprise approximately 200. In recent years, 5-10 disputes have been settled by the conciliation organization at the national level each agreement period, and in the conciliation districts about 10 labour disputes per year. These figures are only indicative, and annual differences can be considerable. There are also marked annual differences in the extent to which the threats of strikes lead to stoppages of work and to what extent work stoppages can be avoided. In some years, only every tenth threat of strike led to a work stoppage, whereas in some years as many as every third of the threats led to a strike. These phenomena are connected, though in a manner difficult to define, with the general labour market atmosphere, the political situation and the economic situation, including employment.

It is possible to stop or to prohibit a strike by the enactment of a special law, which forbids the work stoppage. However, this measure has so far been theoretical, as the conflicts have all ended before any actual legislative measures have been taken. As a rule, the conciliation process is concluded with settlement, although during the past 30 years there have been a few small-scale conflicts which, from just a formal point of view, could still be considered continuing.

It should be noted that the total number of disputes conciliated has been consistently lower when an incomes policy agreement or a centralized labour market settlement covering several years has been in force. In addition, the number of both legal and illegal labour disputes has decreased. This is due, however, more to the factors of change in society than the conciliation mechanisms or relevant legislation.

2.3 Means for the solution of labour conflicts across the community

Conciliation has been used in illegal or political industrial action only exceptionally. In these cases, the methods of conciliation do not follow the Labour Disputes Act and the process is informal. For instance, the conciliator does not present any draft settlement to the parties to be accepted, or at least the settlement proposal is informal.

On a few occasions, employer organizations and some interest groups representing business life have demanded that the Labour Disputes Act be amended by adding a provision allowing a settlement of labour disputes concerning what are called 'key groups' irrespective of the will of the parties to the dispute. For example, in a proposal submitted to the Finnish Government some years ago, the employers' organizations and some other interest groups suggested that the Act be amended by adding a provision under which a tripartite labour dispute board could be appointed with the authority to adopt a labour dispute settlement that would be binding upon the parties to the dispute.[3] In addition, the Confederation of Finnish Industries has recently proposed that an independent investigator should be assigned to settle issues relating to industrial peace. Proposals of this kind have not lead to any concrete measures so far.

2.4 Employment relations in the public sector and in the private sector

Persons employed by the private sector have an employment relationship, whereas those employed by the public sector have mainly a public service relationship, which is an employment relationship governed by public law. Partly legislation of their own and partly labour legislation is applied to the private and public sectors. In recent years, the trend has been towards a unification of the terms of employment.

Both the private and the public sectors partake, if necessary, in incomes-policy or comprehensive labour market negotiations, but the making of collective agreements for the private and the public sectors differ from each other in that the industrial peace agreements of the public sector are made in a centralized way. Local agreement is comprehensive in the public sector.

2.5 Some statistical indicators

Since the Act on Mediation in Labour Disputes came into force in 1962, the number of disputes handled by the national conciliators or district conciliators has varied from six to 200 cases a year. There is no data available on the number of disputes under conciliation where agreement was never reached. An established rule is that if a dispute has been brought to conciliation, settlement will be reached either during the conciliation process or directly between the parties concerned.

3 Tiitinen, Kari-Pekka – Ruponen, Ilkka: *Mediation of the Collective Interest Disputes*. Publication of the Finnish Labour Law Society, No. 1. Helsinki, 1999.

3 Other means of dispute solving

3.1 Arbitration

Arbitration may be substituted for civil proceedings at regular courts, but this almost exclusively happens as regards managerial and comparable employees.

Disputes which would otherwise belong to the jurisdiction of the Labour Court may be referred to arbitration, but this seldom happens. Based on special agreements, arbitration is used to some extent in the graphic industry, communication and media branch as well as in the aviation branch.

In Finland, the use of arbitration in connection with collective agreements is rather limited. In both private and public sectors, it has been adopted almost only in cases where some detail or issue in the collective agreement negotiations has been left open and postponed for later decision in the future. A typical example is a long-term agreement, where the date of a pay raise has been set, but the actual amount of the raise will be agreed upon at a later date during the implementation of the collective agreement. Arbitration has also been practised to some extent both in the private and public sectors for the interpretation of collective agreements.

As earlier mentioned, arbitration can also be a substitute for the Labour Court when the parties concerned, the employers and the trade unions, have agreed on it. In principle, there is no obstacle for concluding the entire collective agreement by arbitration, but as yet the implementation of arbitration has not reached so far.

Arbitration can be implemented in both legal disputes and interest disputes. It is still quite rare in legal individual disputes between an employer and an employee.

The advantage of arbitration is that the parties to the conflict will get a binding decision and industrial peace as a result of the process. The aspect that limits the use of arbitration in concluding collective agreements more widely is the unwillingness of the parties concerned to give their decision making right to such an extent into the hands of outsiders.

There are no statistics available on arbitration in the labour market cases, because arbitration is carried out by many different actors like lawyers and other legal experts.

4 Questionnaire

1. To what extent (if at all) are employment relations in the public sector in your country distinguished from employment relations in the private sector?

Persons employed by the private sector have an employment relationship, whereas those employed by the public sector have mainly a public service relationship, which is an employment relationship governed by public law. Partly legislation of their own and partly labour legislation is applied to the private and public sectors. In recent years, the trend has been towards a unification of the terms of employment.

Both the private and the public sectors partake, if necessary, in incomes-policy or comprehensive labour market negotiations, but the making of collective agreements for the private and the public sectors sector differ from each other in that the industrial peace agreements of the public sector are made in a centralized way. Local agreement is comprehensive in the public sector.

2. In your country, which facilities are provided (by the state and/or both sides of industry) for assisting parties in resolving collective labour disputes (e.g. by offering mediation services)? How do these facilities operate in practice? Do these facilities satisfy a distinct need?

There is a National Conciliators' Office and five conciliation districts for settling disputes of interest, both in the public and private sectors. The parties can, if they want to, set up voluntary conciliation bodies, but these are seldom used. Nor is there any particular legislation on them. Arbitration is used to some extent to solve both interest and legal disputes.

In Finland, the system of labour relations is based mainly on nationwide collective agreements. These comprise approximately 200. In recent years, five to ten disputes have been settled by the conciliation organization at the national level each agreement period, and in the conciliation districts about ten labour disputes per year. These figures are only indicative, and annual differences can be considerable. There are also marked annual differences as to what extent the threats of strikes lead to stoppages of work and to what extent work stoppages can be avoided. In some years, only every tenth threat of strike led to a work stoppage, whereas in some years as many as every third of the threats led to a strike. These phenomena are connected, though in a manner difficult to define, with the general labour market atmosphere, the political situation and the economic situation, including employment.

3. Do facilities differ for the public and private sector respectively?

The conciliation organization of labour disputes in the public and private sector is the same, and the Labour Court is available to both. In the government and municipal sectors, there is also a National Dispute Impact Assessment Board functioning in situations of industrial conflicts. If the Board has deemed the projected stoppage of work to be of such a nature that it leads the essential functions of society into a serious state of disturbance, the Board should exhort the parties to remit the industrial action partly or totally. In no case shall one take any measure submitted to the consideration of the Board earlier than after two weeks from the originally announced date of commencing or extending the projected work stoppage. The Board regularly also takes a stand on the limits to a strike and on their significance with regard to the functions of society.

However, the decision of the Board is a recommendation, and the parties observe it at their discretion.

As to legal proceedings concerning working life, the government and the municipal sectors have their own procedural courses of action. Since the theme of the conference is related to the conciliation of collective interest disputes, these legality disputes are not considered more comprehensively in this connection.

4. In your country, do any restrictions apply to the public sector employees' right to strike? If so, are such restrictions in any way compensated by alternative procedures or options for these employees?

Those employed by the government and in the municipal sector have a more limited right to industrial action than employees in the private sector. The main rule is that work stoppages are prohibited, if they aim to affect anything other than those contractual questions expressly allowed by law. It is not possible to conclude collective agreements on, for instance, the arrangements of the official machinery, the duties of the authorities or internal division of work, the conditions of the eligibility for public offices, pensions and corresponding matters. Therefore these matters may not be promoted by means of industrial action, either.

The only forms of industrial action allowed in the public sector are strikes and lockouts. Sympathy strikes are not allowed at all.

The industrial peace obligation is similar both in the public and private sectors while the collective agreements are valid. In the public sector, the right to strike is very comprehensive. As a rule, only employees functioning as representatives of the employer have no right to resort to industrial action. In addition, in the government sector, the judges of the supreme courts and the whole personnel of the Office of the President of the Republic may not take part in industrial actions.

5. In case the said facilities have been institutionalized (recently), would you say that institutionalization has contributed to a gain in time / a swifter handling of (imminent) disputes?

In the private sector, the present mechanisms of conciliation of labour disputes are based on an Act of 1948, which was revised in 1962. In the public sector, the basis for contractual activity was regulated in 1970.

In recent decades, the number of both legal and illegal labour disputes has decreased. This is due, however, more to the factors of societal changes than the conciliation mechanisms or relevant legislation.

6. Has institutionalization amounted to a restriction of the right to strike?

The right to industrial action has not been limited by legislation or institutionalization in recent decades. The Labour Disputes Act regulates *i.e.* the procedure of giving advance notice of work stoppages.

7. Has institutionalization of mediation as a remedial intervention technique, contributed to the prevention of disputes (e.g. where disputes mediated were identified as symptomatic for underlying, structural problems in a particular company, and advisory work was undertaken by way of follow-up?)

Legislation does not include restraints that would limit preventive measures or the consultation of the parties when labour disputes are imminent. Nowadays it is rather common that the parties turn to the mediating organization even before giving notice of a work stoppage. The success of such voluntary processes depends *i.e.* on the negotiation relations between the parties and on their ability to bear responsibility for their decisions.

If the voluntary mediation process does not lead to any result, and notice of a work stoppage is consequently given, the advantage, however, is that the mediation organization has more a comprehensive understanding of the relevant problems already at the beginning of the mediation.

8. How important do you regard branch-specific knowledge in a mediator?

All knowledge is of course useful, but since the Act on Mediation in Labour Disputes and relevant processes are mainly uniform, one must hold it as a premise that special branch-specific questions are posed to the mediator by the parties. It is in the real interest of the parties to bring forth arguments and facts supporting their stand during the mediation.

9. Against the backdrop of emerging EU collective agreements and genuine European companies, what would be the best way to deal with cross-border collective labour disputes in the nearby future?

This issue was discussed in a particular EU project a few years ago. But the representatives of different countries or the employer and employee parties were not able to reach sufficient agreement on the question. If actual collective agreements at the European level will be made in the future, the matter has to be reconsidered.

10. How should the requirements imposed by Article 6, section 3 of the 1961 European Social Charter be met?

(Art. 6 s. 3 reads: With a view to ensuring the effective exercise of the right to bargain collectively, the Contracting Parties undertake: "[...] to promote the establishment and use of appropriate machinery for conciliation and voluntary arbitration for the settlement of labour disputes".

On Finland's part, no shortcomings as to the application of the said Article (Article 6, Section 3, of the European Social Charter, 1961) have been presented. The text makes it possible to promote conciliation and voluntary arbitration of labour disputes in many alternative ways.

11. How are the facilities in your country being financed? How many staff (fulltime, part-time, other) are involved?

The Finnish conciliation organization is completely financed by the state. The National Conciliator and his secretary are fulltime employees, while the district conciliators (6) function part-time. Voluntary arbitration is funded by the parties.

12. Is there a professional body of knowledge, or are there particular insights, in the areas of dispute resolution and/or collective bargaining that could have relevance for the new EU Member States?

Information concerning the conciliation of labour disputes is available through the Conciliators' Office, the universities and ministries. Additionally, some international studies and summaries have been published. Relevant statutes are also available on the Internet.

CHAPTER 8

The Swedish experience in mediating collective labour disputes

Kurt Eriksson

1 Some background facts

- Sweden depends to a great extent on foreign trade. Exports amount to approximately 44% of the Gross Domestic Product (GDP);
- There are about 4.4 million people in the Swedish labour force, of which some 4.2 million are classified as employees;
- Approximately 70% of Sweden's employees are to be found in the private sector and 30% in the public sector (central government, municipalities and county councils);
- Over 80% of the employees are members of a trade union. A corresponding percentage of employers are affiliated to an employer organization;
- Collective agreements apply to an estimated 90% of the employees. Sweden has no mechanism for the extension of collective agreements. Nor is there any legislation on minimum wages. The percentage of the labour market covered by collective agreements ultimately depends on the level of union activity;
- In general, collective agreements are nationwide industry or sectoral accords, negotiated by national union organizations and employer organizations. At present, there are some 580 collective agreements in force in the Swedish labour market. These regulate such matters as pay and general employment conditions. In addition, there are a number of company-level adjustments via local collective agreements between employers and unions at the workplace;
- On the labour side, there are three peak organizations: the Swedish Trade Union Confederation (*LO*), the Confederation of Professional Employees (*TCO*) and The Swedish Federation of Professional Associations (*SACO*). The *LO* (blue-collar workers) was founded in 1898. Today, it has 1.9 million members in 16 affiliated union organizations. The largest are the Swedish Municipal Workers' Union (570,000 members) and the Swedish Metalworkers' Union (390,000). On the whole, the *LO* member unions share a common structure, with a national head office and local organizations geographically divided into branches, sections and workplace 'clubs' (primarily at large workplaces).
  The *TCO* (white-collar workers), founded in 1944, has 1.3 million members in 18 national union organizations. The largest of these is the Union of Clerical and Technical Employees in Industry (*SIF*), with 365,000 members. The Teachers' Union has 225,000 members. In principle, the white-collar unions are structured in the same way as the blue-collar unions.
  SACO (university trained employees), founded in 1947, has 560,000 members and 29 affiliated union organizations. The largest among them is the Association of Graduate Engineers (*CF*) with 98,000 members. As many *SACO* unions are small, they often lack an organization at the workplace. Instead, members are represented by the national union's local branch.

The *LO* and *TCO* are structured in accordance with the principle of industry-based unionism. This means that a single union organises all employees in the same branch/industry regardless of their professional qualifications or type of employment. *SACO* unions, on the other hand, are organized by profession – such as graduate engineers, doctors, psychologists, and officers;

- The principal organizations on the employer side are the Confederation of Swedish Enterprise, the Swedish Agency for Government Employers and the Swedish Association of Local Authorities and Regions.
  The Confederation of Swedish Enterprise (incorporating the former Swedish Employers Confederation, *SAF*, founded in 1902) is the leading employer organization in the private sector. It comprises 37 industry-based employer associations, representing 54,000 Swedish enterprises with a total labour force of 1.6 million.
  The Swedish Agency for Government Employees is the employer organization for 270 central government agencies with almost 240,000 employees.
  The Swedish Association of Local Authorities and Regions represents 290 municipalities, 18 counties councils and 2 regions. The total number of employees is approximately 1.1 million.
- The social partners in the labour market are sovereign and independent. There is no legislation in Sweden regulating the internal activities of the trade unions or the employer organizations. These activities are regulated by the organizations' statutes, and it is the organizations that decide their content.
  Union activities are financed exclusively out of members' contributions. No government subsidies are provided. Unions are in general financially strong. They own real estate and are shareholders in the stock market. The total market value of the strike funds held by the *LO* and its affiliated unions, for instance, has been estimated at around € 2.2 billion.

2 A historical review

When describing the Swedish system for conflict resolution in the labour market, a look at the historical events that led to the present situation is essential. Firstly, it is important to keep in mind that the differences between the emerging trade union movement in Sweden, in the shape of the *LO*, and the employers organized by the *SAF* never resulted into violent confrontation. The employers never made any serious attempt to crush the union movement. At a fairly early stage, they decided to respect the right of employees to become organized.

The December compromise of 1906

This point of view was manifested in an agreement reached in 1906 between the *LO* and the *SAF*, known as the 'December compromise'. The *SAF* recognised the *LO* as an organization and acknowledged the workers' absolute right to organize themselves in trade unions. The right to organize paved the way for the right to negotiate. The *LO* for its part accepted the employers' right to freely hire and fire workers and to exercise managerial command of Swedish enterprises. Ever since that date, the employers have never questioned the right of employees to organize (right of association). This compromise gave birth to the spirit of co-operation and consensus that subsequently informed the relationship between the social partners, and which developed further and reached its peak in the 1950s and 1960s.

The December compromise enabled the partners to avert the introduction of extensive legislation planned by the government of the day. The only legislative outcome was a 1906 law on mediation in industrial disputes, compliance with which was entirely voluntary. A special authority, the National Conciliator's Office, was established to administer mediation activities. In 1920, the law was made more stringent in certain respects, but voluntary participation remained the basic principle.

The Collective Agreement Act and the Labour Court

The *SAF*'s recognition of the workers' right of association paved the way for the development of collective agreements. In certain respects, however, there was confusion as to their legal status. The key issue was the extent to which agreements were binding. This was of crucial importance for the right of workers to take industrial action during a current contractual period. The 1928 Collective Agreement Act laid down that collective agreements are binding upon both the contracting organizations and their members. Employers and employees bound by collective agreements cannot legitimately enter into contractual obligations that conflict with the collective agreement. In addition, the law prescribed that industrial action aimed at bringing about a change in a collective agreement was not allowed during the contractual period. These rules still apply. In the same year, the Labour Court was established in Sweden. Its principal task was and still is to settle disputes of rights (legal disputes) between organizations in the labour market concerning the interpretation and implementation of collective agreements and new laws.

Further legislation was introduced in 1936. The aim was to make it easier for white-collar workers to organize, as they had encountered the same kind of resistance from employers as the workers had 40 years earlier. The Act on the Right to Organise and Negotiate introduced in that year meant that white-collar professionals were entitled to belong to a union organization and to promote union activity. The law was incumbent on both employers and employees.

The Saltsjöbaden Agreement of 1938

The second epoch-making agreement between the *LO* and the *SAF*, the *Saltsjöbaden* Agreement, was signed in 1938. As in the case of the 1906 December compromise, it was brought on by government plans for wide-ranging employment legislation. This time round, the document was about industrial action, neutrality and disputes that threaten the public interest. During the first half of the 1930s, Sweden experienced some 700 labour disputes a year, which led to calls for legislative action. The *LO* and the *SAF* shared the view that conditions in the labour market should be regulated by the partners themselves without any political interference. The twin aims of the agreement were to prevent the introduction of new legislation – which it succeeded in doing – and to reduce the frequency of disputes. The *Saltsjöbaden* Agreement is basically still in force and has served as a model for similar agreements in other sectors of the labour market. It is principally a peace document. However, the manner in which it was formulated has invested it with much greater influence. It introduced binding rules on orderly negotiating procedures in pursuit of collective agreements, which must be followed before industrial action can be taken. The agreement also contains rules to protect neutral third parties, rules on grievance handling, and rules on disputes threatening the public interest and on ways of avoiding them.

Centralised bargaining

The *Saltsjöbaden* Agreement paved the way for the co-operation between the *LO* and the *SAF* that subsequently developed in a number of different areas. The negotiating system was centralised. Between 1956 and 1982, negotiations on new collective agreements on pay and employment conditions for blue-collar workers followed the same pattern. The negotiations were in three stages. First, the *LO* and the *SAF* agreed on the economic framework and advised their member organizations to adopt it in the form of collective agreements. The organizations then formally concluded such agreements incorporating the terms agreed on by the *LO* and the *SAF*. Finally, the details were settled in company-level agreements between the two sides.

In the early 1970s, a negotiating cartel was established comprising unions in the *TCO* and SACO spheres operating in the private sector. This was the Federation of Salaried Employees in Industry and Services (*PTK*), and it became the white-collar equivalent of the *LO* in negotiations with the *SAF*. On certain occasions, the *LO* and the *PTK* joined forces at the negotiating table.

The public sector expands and wage formation breaks down

During the 1960s and 1970s, the Swedish public sector expanded, and the workforce grew substantially. Once primarily the remit of the partners in the private sector, wage formation now became a matter for the organizations representing public employees as well. An important event that came to affect and gradually complicate wage negotiations in the private sector was the introduction of a law in 1965 granting public employees the right to negotiate and strike. The unions in this sector came to display a militancy that was in contrast to the spirit of co-operation that had developed between the *LO* and the *SAF*. The resultant growth in public wages caused the *LO* unions to adjust their wage demands upwards, and in time a wage spiral developed. As soon as an organization had succeeded in its negotiating aims, other organizations demanded more. This race for higher wages, combined with a slowdown in economic growth, created an increasing disparity between nominal and real wage levels. Higher nominal wage increases than were to be found in the outside world drove up the inflation rate and eroded real wages. Despite wage increases totalling 150%, real wages did not increase at all between 1980 and 1995. To avert collapse in the employment sector, Sweden was forced to devaluate, which further boosted the inflation rate.

Laws on job security and co-determination

In the early 1970s, a political turnaround *vis-à-vis* the labour market occurred in Sweden. The previous approach whereby it was left to the social partners to settle their differences through collective agreements without any state interference gave way to a government policy of instituting change through legislation. This primarily concerned matters relating to job security and co-determination for workers in the employer's decision-making process. Despite employer opposition to legislative action, the *Riksdag* (Swedish parliament) was virtually unanimous in adopting the Security of Employment Act (1974) and the Co-Determination Act (1976). The provisions from 1928 concerning collective agreements and industrial action were incorporated into the latter law, as were the rules from 1936 concerning the right to organize and negotiate. The 1920 law on mediation was also incorporated, with some minor adjustments. In addition, a number of provisions were introduced aimed at giving the workplace unions a say in employer decision-making. One such rule was that before making a decision involving any substantial change in the company's operations or seriously affecting the employees, employers must of their own accord into negotiations with the union organization at the workplace with which he is bound to negotiate pursuant to a collective agreement.

Some researchers and other observers have described this provision as the first step towards the phase-out of what has come to be known as the 'Swedish model'. It upset the balance between the social partners, and the state no longer took a neutral position. The *SAF* asked whether there was any point in concluding collective agreements if the outcome could later be altered by state intervention.

The end of centralised bargaining

A few years later, the system of collective negotiations between the *LO* and the *SAF* began to erode. Following a large-scale dispute that spread throughout the labour market in 1980, the Swedish Association of Engineering Employers refused to give the *SAF* a mandate to negotiate. Instead, in 1983, it reached an agreement in direct negotiation with its counterpart, the Swedish Metalworkers' Union. Other employer organizations in the *SAF* followed suit, and this signalled the end of centralized negotiations in the private sector. The present order soon became general practice, involving direct wage negotiations between employers and unions at national industry/sectoral level.

Measures to save the economy – temporary solutions

As noted above, the 1980s and 1990s were difficult times for the Swedish economy. Inefficient wage formation has been described as a major factor. The problems had their roots in the mid-1970s, when wages began to rise faster than productivity. Wage increases were eaten up by inflation. The Swedish Government sought to remedy the situation by means of a series of devaluations. It abandoned this policy in the mid-1980s, however, deciding that such a strategy was not sustainable in the long term.

In 1990, the government proposed a two-year moratorium on prices and wages and the prohibition of strikes. The aim was to gain control over wage and cost development in the labour market. The proposals, however, were rejected by the *Riksdag*. The government resigned, re-formed and adopted a new strategy. Instead of legislating, it sought to persuade the social partners to assume greater responsibility for their actions. The government appointed a negotiating group comprising experienced negotiators and mediators. The group's task was to try to achieve a downward shift in cost trends. It succeeded in this aim by persuading the social partners in 1991 to accept a two-year 'stabilisation pact'. This settlement involved a centralized package solution under which the partners agreed to wind down wages and costs.

Collaboration agreements between the industrial partners

The 1995 bargaining round in Sweden led once again to higher wage cost increases than the economy could stand. At the same time, unemployment was relatively high by Swedish standards. The government became concerned once again at how wage formation was developing. In the spring of 1996, it invited the partners to join together to draw up the changes that were required in the wage formation system, by March 1997 at the latest. At national level, the partners, *i.e.* the peak organizations, failed to agree on a common set of proposals. However, the partners in the industrial sector (12 employer associations and seven unions) agreed in March 1997 to co-operate more closely. This agreement – known as the Industrial Agreement – encompasses two parts: the Agreement on Industrial Development and Wage Formation and the Agreement on Industrial Bargaining Procedure. Three different bodies are attached to the agreement, including mediators, with the task of assisting the partners at the negotiating table. In general, the purpose of the Industrial Agreement is to promote industrial development, profitability and competitiveness and thus pave the way for favourable wage growth for employees. In addition, the aim is to create a situation in which the industrial partners can avoid industrial action and engage in constructive wage negotiations resulting in balanced settlements.

The 1998 round of bargaining was completed virtually without any disputes and resulted in moderate wage increases. The Industrial Agreement could fairly be described as a major factor in this development.

Efforts to develop rules acceptable to both sides

In April 1997, the government appointed a special investigator to recommend ways of strengthening the state mediation body and to review the rules on industrial disputes. The investigator's report, presented in November 1998, met with mixed reactions from the social partners. The unions were particularly concerned about the proposed restrictions on the rules relating to industrial action.

In 1999, the government appointed former Prime Minister Ingvar Carlsson to examine the prospects for getting the partners to agree on a common set of rules concerning wage formation. He found that the partners had widely differing views on how these rules ought to be formulated, but shared a degree of consensus on certain principles in relation to wage formation. They agreed, for instance, that a mediation body was both necessary and needed strengthening, and they welcomed the idea of completing negotiations in the internationally competitive areas first, as long as negotiations in other bargaining areas could proceed at the same time.

Establishment of the National Mediation Office

As the peak organizations in the labour market could not agree on a set of rules, the government had no option but to take the legislative route. The National Mediation Office was set up on 1 June 2000. At the same time, the National Conciliator's Office was closed down after almost a century in operation.

The National Mediation Office is a government agency, and its duties are defined more explicitly in the Co-Determination Act and in a special ordinance. The agency is required by law to promote an efficient wage formation process and to mediate in labour disputes. The former task is a new one in the Swedish mediation field. Previously, the emphasis was on ensuring industrial peace, while the socio-economic consequences of wage agreements were of secondary interest. The reasons given for introducing the legislative changes were that wage formation had not worked satisfactorily for several decades, both from a societal perspective and from the perspective of the individual wage earner. The unions (*TCO* and *SACO*) criticized the proposals. They felt the changes were too drastic and represented interference with the free right of negotiation. They also expressed concern at the prospect of a stronger element of state income policy in the collective bargaining process.

Besides providing for the establishment of the National Mediation Office, the Co-Determination Act laid down a number of rules concerning the agency's powers to act in specific situations, and also incorporated a more detailed description of its duties. To a great extent, the new rules in the Swedish labour market were inspired by those in the above-mentioned Industrial Agreement.

The division of roles between the state and the social partners

In its bill introducing the legislative changes, the government described the division of roles between the state and the social partners in the following terms. The chief responsibility for wage formation lies with the social partners. The state, however, has overall responsibility for the economy, and is also responsible for representing the interests of groups excluded from the labour market. The wage formation process as a whole must not lead to unsustainable outcomes that make the creation of new jobs more difficult.

The government then developed this line of argument and added. In Sweden, the social partners themselves have long been responsible for concluding wage agreements in the labour market, without interference from the government or the *Riksdag*. The free right of negotiation is a cornerstone of the Swedish labour market. The employees' right to strike and the employers' right to impose lockouts are both enshrined in the constitution. This fundamental principle of wage formation is to remain in place. The chief responsibility for wage formation will continue to lie with the social partners.

The state is to adopt a neutral position in relation to the social partners. The scale of wage increases and their distribution among the different employee groups is to be settled by negotiation. But the public interest must also be taken into account in the wage formation process. Employees must have the right to fight for their relative pay levels and employers must have the right to act in support of their views on how wage formation should proceed – but the result must not be wage inflation and fewer jobs.

Collaboration agreements with negotiation arrangements in new areas

In 2001, much of the Swedish labour market, including the whole of the public sector, entered into collaboration agreements on negotiation arrangements (bargaining procedure) similar to the one in the Industrial Agreement. Today, half of the country's employees are covered by agreements of this kind. However, far fewer than half of the 580-odd national industry/sectoral agreements on pay and employment conditions are negotiated within such a framework. Today, about 100 industry-level collective agreements are in force between parties bound by agreements on negotiation arrangements. That leaves roughly 450 agreements to be negotiated within the framework of the Co-Determination Act and thereby potential disputes for the National Mediation Office to deal with.

The LO and the SAF resume negotiations

The aim of such agreements is to help solve adjustment problems when a company experiences a work shortage. Those laid off are to be given both financial assistance and support in their search for fresh work. These accords have been adopted by the parties at national level in the form of collective agreements. There is nothing to suggest, however, that their member organizations would be prepared to issue the *LO* and the Confederation of Swedish Enterprises with a mandate to negotiate on pay as well.

3 The duties of the National Mediation Office in greater detail

The National Mediation Office is required by law to perform two main tasks. One is to mediate in labour disputes. The other is to promote an efficient wage formation process. Both require the agency to keep abreast of forthcoming or current negotiations on pay and employment conditions, either through talks with the parties concerned or by other means. The agency is also required to provide guidance and information to the social partners on negotiations and collective agreements.

3.1 Promoting an efficient wage formation process

A number of new factors affect wage formation in Sweden:

- an independent *Riksbank* (Swedish Central Bank) is now required to pursue a low-inflation policy. Interest rates are to be raised to offset excessively large pay increases. The bank has set an inflation goal of 2% (+ – 1%) per annum;
- a floating rate of exchange was introduced in 1992 for the Swedish currency, the *krona*. Together with the low-inflation policy pursued by the *Riksbank*, this means that excessively large pay increases are offset by interest rate increases, leading to lower growth and lower employment trends than would otherwise have been the case;
- internationalization is affecting the Swedish economy;
- the social partners in Sweden have assumed greater responsibility for wage formation by reaching special collaboration agreements on negotiation arrangements. The first such accord was the above-mentioned Agreement on Industrial Development and Wage Formation, concluded in 1997. Since then, similar agreements have been signed between the parties in the public sector;
- Sweden is moving towards a decentralized and individualized system of wage formation. In many areas, agreements have been reached that make no reference to centrally negotiated pay structures – everything is decided at the local workplace. Most agreements, however, still incorporate stipulated guarantees regarding the minimum pay rise for each individual.

There are a number of dimensions involved. One is that between private and public activities, while another is that between the competitive sector and activities that are not exposed to international competition. A third dimension is that between occupations dominated by women and men respectively, and a fourth is that between low- and high-income earners.

The chief responsibility for wage formation lies with the social partners. The National Mediation Office's duty to promote an efficient wage formation process means it must work in various ways to help the negotiating parties pay due regard to the macro-economic situation. When establishing the agency, the government declared that a low rate of inflation and a high rate of employment growth were required if its employment targets were to be achieved. It also specified that wage formation should provide for real wage growth for employees without causing cost levels in Sweden to exceed those of its major competitors.

In its instructions to the National Mediation Office, the government specified the main objectives in pursuit of an efficient wage formation process. They are:

- to actively seek the development of timetables for the bargaining process with the aim of reaching new agreements before the previous contractual period expires. The aim of such a course is to avert industrial action;
- to consult with the parties on bargaining prospects in light of the macro-economic situation;
- to fully exploit and uphold the consensus that exists in the Swedish labour market on the pattern-setting role of the competitive sector in pay negotiations. This is to be achieved through direct talks with the parties concerned;
- to collect, compile and interpret statistics of importance for wage formation and also to analyze those collective agreements deemed to be of interest in this respect.

In this connection, it should be noted that the National Mediation Office has overall responsibility for the official Swedish wage statistics, which are produced by Statistics Sweden (*SCB*). The agency's task is to commission statistics that as far as possible will meet the needs of the various users.

The National Mediation Office is required to promote an efficient wage formation process, in respect of all parties in the labour market regardless of whether they have entered into agreements on negotiation arrangements. However, the agency has only limited powers for mediating between parties bound by such agreements. Before describing the rules on mediation, therefore, it is worth taking a closer look at this type of agreement.

3.2 Agreements on negotiation arrangements

Bargaining areas with agreements on negotiation arrangements

A relatively new phenomenon in the Swedish labour market is the fact that the partners at sectoral or industrial level have increasingly concluded agreements on the forms for bargaining, generally known as agreements on negotiation arrangements. The Agreement on Industrial Development and

Wage Formation mentioned above is an example in point. It contains a timetable, the purpose of which is to ensure that bargaining gets under way in time for a new collective agreement to be negotiated before the old one expires. A timetable may stipulate for instance that bargaining is to begin three months prior to the expiry of the current agreement and that the talks are to be led by an impartial chair. The task of the impartial chair is to assist the parties in the negotiations should they fail to reach agreement among themselves. The chair is empowered to order the parties to examine and identify individual bargaining issues. Further, chairs may present proposals of their own for a solution to the issues in hand. They are also entitled to order a cooling-off period for previously notified industrial action until such time as all possible avenues have been explored in search of a solution, but for no longer than 14 calendar days. In addition, an economic advisory council of four independent experts has been attached to the parties in the above-mentioned collaboration agreement. The council's task is to issue statements and recommendations on economic matters.

The collaboration agreement in the industrial sector has been followed by similar accords elsewhere. Such agreements now apply throughout the local and regional government sector. The Swedish state, too, has concluded collaboration agreements with its counterparts, via the Agency for Government Employees.

Bargaining areas without agreements on negotiation arrangements

Although agreements on negotiation arrangements are in place in several major areas, they are not to be found everywhere. Among the major bargaining areas that lack such accords are the retail trade, the construction industry and the transport industry.

3.3 Mediation in the bargaining process

The National Mediation Office conducts its activities on two levels. In both cases, the work involves mediating in disputes between parties with differing interests, but the actual mediation process operates at different levels. The most important is the one at which national organizations negotiate nationwide agreements at industry level or sectoral level. As noted earlier, there are some 520 nationwide collective agreements in force in the Swedish labour market. Mediators in these negotiations are appointed on an *ad hoc* basis. In addition, the National Mediation Office has six regional mediators at its disposal on a permanent basis. Their task is to mediate in collective bargaining between non-organized employers and the union. As a rule, this form of mediation appears when a union seeks to pressure an employer into signing a collective agreement (an accession agreement) by giving notice of industrial action.

Voluntary mediation

If the parties negotiating collective agreements accept such a course, the National Mediation Office may appoint negotiation managers or mediators to join the bargaining process. In practice, this involves one or both of the parties requesting assistance and formally asking the National Mediation Office to proceed with such an appointment. Should one of the parties oppose such a course, the National Mediation Office is prevented from appointing a negotiation manager or a mediator.

Compulsory mediation

Should the National Mediation Office decide that a risk of industrial action is present, or if such action has already been initiated, the agency may appoint a mediator without the consent of the parties concerned. Under the Co-Determination Act, a party intending to take industrial action has to notify the other side in writing and also submit written notification to the National Mediation Office no later than seven working days in advance. Once notification has been received, the National Mediation Office assumes that there is a risk of industrial action but does not necessarily appoint mediators immediately. The situation may be such that there is little prospect of a mediator being able to achieve results. In such cases, the National Mediation Office refrains from taking an immediate decision and monitors developments instead.

Parties with agreements on negotiation arrangements – *i.e.* agreements on bargaining procedure that contain timetables for negotiations, time frames and rules for the appointment of mediators, rules on mediators' powers of authority and rules on the termination of agreements – are exempted from the regulations concerning compulsory mediation. This however is conditional upon the parties having reported the agreement to the National Mediation Office and the agency having registered it. In such cases, the National Mediation Office may not prescribe compulsory mediation. This is because the parties in such agreements should not have to be bound by dual systems.

Mediators appointed by the National Mediation Office

The task of a mediator is to seek agreement between the parties. To this end, the mediator is required to summon the parties to the negotiating table or to take appropriate action of some other kind. Parties summoned to negotiations by a mediator are duty bound to attend. Should any party fail to appear or fail to take part in some other way, the mediator may ask the National Mediation Office to require the party concerned to fulfil its obligations on penalty of a fine.

To help settle disputes satisfactorily, mediators can put forward their own proposals for a settlement. A mediator may also recommend that the two sides settle their dispute by arbitration. The mediator, however, cannot compel them to take such a step. Arbitration presupposes the agreement of both sides. It is not enough for one of the parties to accept such a procedure. The National Mediation Office can appeal to disputants to settle matters by arbitration. Nevertheless, the agency, too, lacks the power to enforce such a step.

Only very rarely do the parties involved refer a dispute of interest to arbitration. This has only happened once or twice in the past ten years, and then only in relation to a minor issue. Disputes over the size of pay increases at branch or sectoral level are not settled by arbitration.

Mediators must also seek to persuade the party concerned to postpone or cancel a planned industrial action. Should the party refuse to comply with the mediator's request to postpone an action for which notice has been given, the mediator may request the National Mediation Office to order the party concerned to postpone it. Should the agency decide that such a course would help bring about a satisfactory settlement to the dispute, it may order a postponement. An industrial action may only be postponed for 14 days at the most, and such a course may only be taken once per term of mediation. The National Mediation Office does not have the power to call off industrial action already under way. Such powers would be in violation of Sweden's commitments under international conventions.

4 Questionnaire

1. Employment relations in the public and private sectors

Relying on the responsible behaviour of the social partners could be described as a distinguishing feature of the Swedish bargaining system. In line with this outlook, measures were taken to reduce the gap between private and public sectors, starting with the introduction of the 1965 law that gave public employees the right to strike and to negotiate. This meant that relations between the parties in the public sector corresponded more closely to those that applied in the private sector. With the introduction of the Co-Determination Act in 1976, the right of negotiation came to apply throughout the labour market to all aspects of the 'labour-management relationship'. The Public Employment Act was introduced at the same time, laying down special rules for the public sector. Overall, however, only minor differences remained between the private and the public sector. The rules governing industrial disputes are one such difference that still applies. However, the similarities between the private and public sectors in this respect are greater than the differences. The general view is that the parties in the public sector – under present laws and agreements – have an extensive right of negotiation and with only a few restrictions have the right to take industrial action to put pressure on the opposing side in negotiations.

2. Facilities provided for assisting parties in resolving collective labour disputes

Collective labour disputes can be divided into two categories: disputes of interest and disputes of rights (legal disputes). The mechanisms for solving disputes are dependent on which type of dispute is involved. A principle that is common to all types of disputes is that the parties are to seek a solution through negotiation.

In the case of disputes of rights, *i.e.* disputes over the interpretation or implementation of a particular law or agreement, this principle is laid down in collective agreements and in the Co-Determination Act. Should the parties fail in this endeavour, the final decision rests with the Labour Court. No industrial action is allowed in cases involving disputes of rights. Nor does the National Mediation Office appoint mediators in such cases. The Labour Court, however, is required to take active steps to help the parties arrive at a settlement, insofar as this is deemed appropriate, bearing in mind the nature of the case and other circumstances.

Disputes of interest concern what is to apply between the parties in the future, *e.g.* the substance of a collective agreement that the parties are negotiating. It is this type of dispute on which the National Mediation Office focuses its attention, as the agency's goal is industrial peace. If the parties fail to reach a new collective agreement before the old one expires, bargaining takes place without any obligation to maintain peaceful industrial relations, which means the parties are free to take industrial action in support of their demands.

The basic principle is that mediation is voluntary. Should both parties – generally those engaged in negotiating new collective agreements at industry/sectoral level – agree on the need to call in mediators, the National Mediation Office immediately complies with their request. In cases where only one party requests mediation, the National Mediation Office contacts the other party to learn its views. In most cases, a consensus is reached and mediators are appointed.

A party intending to take industrial action is required by law to notify both the other party and the National Mediation Office no later than seven working days in advance. When the agency receives such notification, it immediately contacts the parties to determine whether they are agreed on the need for mediation, which they usually are nowadays. Mediators are then appointed, normally as soon as the parties agree that mediation is required.

Under Swedish law, further assistance is available to negotiating parties. If they agree on such a course, the National Mediation Office can appoint 'negotiation managers', who lead the talks from an early stage, before a dispute has developed. The agency usually suggests introducing negotiation managers when communicating with parties who traditionally find it difficult to reach a settlement without mediation.

The costs of using negotiation managers and mediators are paid by the state. No charge is made to the parties involved. In cases where agreements on negotiation arrangements (bargaining procedure) apply, the parties have usually decided that mediators are to be brought into the talks a month prior to the expiry of the current collective agreement.

3. The public and private sectors

The activities of the National Mediation Office range across the entire labour market. The law makes no distinction between public and private sector. The parties in the public sector, however, have concluded agreements on negotiation arrangements, and these have been registered with the National Mediation Office. The reason is that these parties shared a common desire to conduct their negotiations themselves and to appoint their own mediators should such a move prove necessary.

4. Public employees' right to strike

Public employees in Sweden have a wide-ranging right to negotiate and to take industrial action. As noted above, the Co-Determination Act also applies in the public sector. When this law was introduced, however, it was accompanied by a special piece of legislation, the Public Employment Act, which imposed certain restrictions on the right to co-determination and the right to take industrial action in the public sector. This was replaced by a new Public Employment Act in 1994.

The Special Basic Agreement for the Public Sector in 1976 is an accord designed to protect the country's political system. The parties to it are all the relevant union and employer organizations at central, regional and local government levels. Under this agreement, the parties are required to strive for peaceful negotiations and avoid industrial action over issues that they are deemed incapable of settling without encroaching upon political democracy in the country. These include issues relating to the objectives, direction, extent and quality of public activities. The parties have also set up a Special Board for the Public Sector, whose task is to make recommendations on delimitation issues under the agreement. During its 30 years of existence, this body has had to settle only one issue, which suggests that the parties have taken pains to avoid demands that may conflict with political democracy in Sweden.

The Public Employment Act

This law contains special provisions on labour disputes. These rules are binding and cannot be negated by collective agreements. The Public Employment Act applies both to national agencies answerable to the government and to the *Riksdag* and its agencies. The law's special provisions on labour disputes, however, also apply to municipal and county council employees.

The Public Employment Act limits the scope for industrial action in connection with the exercise of public authority. This refers to the exercise of official power in relation to the benefits, rights and obligations of the individual. Such matters are settled by means of binding unilateral decisions by a public authority on the basis of a public law statute. A typical example of the exercise of public authority is the administration of justice, *e.g.* certain decisions handed down by judicial, police or executive bodies. Other examples are the granting of benefits and allowances of various kinds, the admission of pupils and students, the enforcement of regulations, and public inspections of buildings and food outlets, *etc.*

In the case of work relating to the exercise of such authority, industrial action is only allowed in the form of lockouts, strikes, blockades on overtime or blockades on recruitment. Other industrial actions such as partial strikes, sit-down strikes, go-slow actions, refusal to travel, etc, are prohibited for people in this type of employment. Thus the law distinguishes between the exercise of public authority and other labour market activities. In the case of public activities other than the exercise of public authority, the rules in the Co-Determination Act concerning industrial action apply.

In the case of work relating to the exercise of public authority, industrial action is subject to further restrictions. Sympathy action may not be taken in support of parties in the private labour market. In addition, industrial action aimed at influencing political relations within the country is prohibited. This applies both to the exercise of public authority and to other forms of public activity.

In the event of a dispute over whether a certain type of industrial action is permitted under the Public Employment Act, the action may not be taken until the dispute has been finally settled by the Labour Court. The legislators' aim is to prevent an unlawful type of industrial action being launched as the result of a failure to interpret the legal situation properly.

5. *Has institutionalization saved time or contributed to a swifter handling of (imminent) disputes?*

In 2000, the National Conciliator's Office was replaced by the National Mediation Office, and the new agency was invested with additional tasks and powers. A fundamental aim was to bring the agency into the bargaining process early on and engage the parties in a discussion on the macro-economic conditions for wage formation. At the same time, the agency was to identify potential areas of conflict between the parties and offer assistance in the form of negotiation managers or mediators. As mentioned earlier, much of the new legislation was inspired by the Industrial Agreement, where the parties themselves had drawn up a regulatory framework for their negotiations and attached permanent mediators (designated 'impartial chairs') to their negotiating teams.

A new feature of the legislation was the scope given to the parties to organize their mediation activities themselves via agreements on negotiation arrangements, and thus avoid the need for compulsory mediation ordered by the National Mediation Office. The requirement is that such agreements must contain timetables for bargaining, time frames and rules for the appointment of mediators, rules concerning the powers of the mediators, and rules on the termination of agreements. If these requirements are met, the parties can register the agreement with the National Mediation Office. Today, 18 such agreements are registered with the agency. Often, all parties in a particular industry or sector have signed a joint agreement in this respect. As a result, there are now agreements on negotiation arrangements in force throughout the public sector and the industrial sector, and in a number of service industries. A distinguishing feature of these agreements is that they contain common goals with regard to wage formation. The agreements concluded in the private sector, for instance, state that the aim is to maintain competitiveness in the industry concerned. The agreement governing the state sector asserts that wage bargaining outcomes are to "[...] help bring about macro-economic balance and not upset the efforts of competitive enterprise to maintain cost levels that correspond to those in the outside world."

Another point worth mentioning is that the agreements include timetables for bargaining and a clearly stated ambition to conclude a new collective agreement before the old one expires. This is in line with the National Mediation Office's mandate to promote the development of timetables for collective bargaining that provide for the signing of new agreements before the end of the current contractual period.

It may seem strange that the Swedish state, having set up the National Mediation Office to promote an efficient wage formation process and take a firmer grip on mediation activities, then allows the parties to create their own systems via collective agreements alongside the state system. This is due to the deeply-rooted Swedish belief that collective agreements are preferable to legislation, and to awareness that the parties in the labour market assume joint responsibility for the outcome. The state, however, has not given the parties free rein in shaping their own systems. An agreement concerning negotiation arrangements cannot be officially registered unless it meets the quality requirements laid down by the law.

In 2001, collective agreements on pay and employment conditions were reached on behalf of most of the private sector in Sweden. These agreements were of three years' duration, and bargaining on new agreements took place in 2004. The same process occurred in the state sector. In all, some 420 new nationwide collective agreements were concluded at industry and sectoral levels in 2004. Over 70% of these were finalized before or directly in conjunction with the expiry of the previous agreement.

In 24 sets of negotiations, mediation was required before a new collective agreement could be reached. In 15 of these 24 cases, notice was given of industrial action. In four of these, industrial action was taken. With one exception, the action lasted for only a short period.

The establishment of the National Mediation Office and the advent of agreements on negotiation arrangements have led to a situation in which new collective agreements are largely concluded before the old ones expire. This means that the risk of conflicts in connection with bargaining rounds has been reduced, as industrial action is not permitted while the parties are bound by collective agreements.

As a result of its regular contact with the parties to the labour market, the National Mediation Office is able to offer assistance in the form of negotiation managers or mediators in the early stages of the bargaining process. In addition, the parties are required to notify the agency of pending industrial action. In principle, mediators are appointed on the same day as the agency receives notification of such action. This means that the mediators have about a week in which to try to avert the conflict by helping the parties to reach a settlement and sign a new contract. They usually succeed in this endeavour.

6. Restrictions on the right to strike?

The establishment of the National Mediation Office has not affected the parties' right to take industrial action. The basic legislation from 1976 still applies in its original form. The legislative changes introduced in 2000 were not aimed at restricting the right to take industrial action. The aim was to provide the parties with additional support at an early stage in the bargaining process and help them reach peaceful settlements at wage levels that were acceptable in macro-economic terms.

The National Mediation Office's enhanced authority does not mean restrictions on the right to strike as such. The agency can delay the start of an industrial action. The power to decide on compulsory mediation and a cooling-off period are rather means to put pressure on the bargaining parties – together with the mediators – to explore all possibilities to an amicable settlement of the dispute. If they fail, the parties are free to start the notified industrial action.

7. Contribution to conflict prevention?

As noted earlier, the activities of the National Mediation Office are directed at the parties engaged in negotiating agreements at the national level. Disputes of interest at company level – except in the case of union demands for collective agreements with non-organized employers – are not dealt with by the National Mediation Office. Mediation, then, is confined almost exclusively to collective bargaining between organizations. These are represented by professional negotiators, which mean that areas under dispute have generally been thoroughly analysed and discussed before the mediators come onto the scene. Frequently, there are issues which are so complicated that they cannot be resolved within the framework of a mediation assignment. In such cases, the parties usually agree to remove the issue from the mediation agenda and refer it to a joint working group whose task is to develop proposals for solving the problem during the current contractual period. On occasion, mediators are appointed by the parties to chair such working groups.

8. The importance of industry-specific expertise in a mediator

The National Mediation Office has at its disposal a group of about 30 *ad hoc* mediators, representing a solid blend of experts. The majority are retired senior negotiators from the labour market organizations. A number of former cabinet ministers and senior government officials are also in the group. Two mediators are appointed for each individual assignment or three if the dispute is a major one.

The parties seldom require the mediators to have expert knowledge of the industry concerned. Rather, they are interested in the mediators' experience in previous negotiations and of their ability to find solutions to difficult problems. As a rule, the parties inform the mediators about relations and problems in their particular industry during the initial stages of the process. Sometimes, however, parties who have previously had experience with specific mediators express a preference to use them again when a new dispute arises. Often, the prime reason is not that the mediators have gained an insight into the workings of that particular industry, but rather that they are familiar with how the agreement in question operates.

9. *Financing and staff*

The activities of the National Mediation Office are financed out of the national budget. The *ad hoc* mediators appointed by the agency are paid per assignment in accordance with a fixed hourly fee. The regular regional mediators attached to the agency are paid a monthly remuneration.

In the government bill establishing the National Mediation Office, it was stated that the staff were to be skilled in economics, wage formation, collective bargaining, labour law, pay statistics, contract interpretation and gender equality. Today, there are nine staff members who together possess the skills laid down in the bill. In addition, the agency has two special advisors at its disposal: an economist and an experienced mediator.

Finally, the National Mediation Office organizes a number of conferences and seminars for its mediators each year, focusing on such matters as the macroeconomic conditions for wage formation, bargaining outcomes and specific mediation cases.

CHAPTER 9

The Spanish system of extrajudicial settlements in collective conflict[1]

Fernando Valdés Dal-Ré

1 Multi-industry agreements for extrajudicial settlement of conflicts: their strategic value

The Spanish system of labour relations underwent, during the middle years of the nineteen nineties, an increase of *au sommet* collective bargaining. In other words, social dialogue at the highest levels underwent a significant change. In a period of just five years (December 1992 to April 1997), the most representative trade union organizations and employers' associations at the national level[2] signed more than half a dozen multi-industry agreements on issues with a high strategic value,[3] thereby recovering the leadership in the organization of the Spanish system of labour relations, reinforcing and stressing their autonomous aspects. The I Agreement on Extrajudicial Settlement of Conflicts (ASEC) also belongs to this generation of multi-industry agreements and was signed in January 1996 with two later renewals: in January 2001 (II ASEC) and in December 2005 (III ASEC) were signed.[4]

Assessing this significant effort towards bargaining from a systematic and global perspective, I ASEC and AINC were the agreements equipped with a greater strategic value. With their negotiation and signing, both sides of industry expressed a resolute design to intervene in the basic structures of the Spanish system of labour relations with its conformation in view. Both agreements, I ASEC and AINC, constitute key pieces in a complex social engineering process aimed at redefining the current model of labour relations, making social dialogue the path of legal regulation *par excellence*. In short, the implicit proposal was to install collective bargaining at the core of the Spanish system of

1 Abbreviations: ACV (Agreement on the Coverage of Legal Voids); AIEE (Inter-confederate Agreement on Employment Stability); AINC (Inter-confederate Agreement on Collective Bargaining); ANC (National Agreement on Collective Bargaining); ANFC (National Agreement on Continuous Training); AIOR (Inter-confederate Agreement on issues of Labour Bylaws and Labour Regulations); ASEC (Agreement for the Extrajudicial Settlement of Labour Conflict); CC.OO. (Comisiones Obreras, Spanish Trade Union); CEOE (Spanish Confederation of Employers' Organizations); CEPYME (Spanish Confederation of Small and Medium Enterprises); CES (Economic and Social Council); CP (Peer Commission); ET (Workers' Statute Law); LPL (Labour Procedure Law) and UGT (Unión General de Trabajadores, Spanish Trade Union).

2 The signing parties were CC.OO and UGT, on the trade union side, and CEOE and CEPYME, on the employers' side.

3 The agreements signed were: I ANFC (16-12-1992), II ANFC (19-12-1996), AIOR (7-10-1994) and AIEE, AINC and ACV, all on April 1997.

4 The amendments introduced in II ASEC with respect to I ASEC can be qualified, in general, as technical adjustments. Furthermore, III ASEC, which is currently in force, carried out the merging into a single text of two documents; the ASEC itself and its Regulations. In accordance with what is stated in Art. 2.2 of III ASEC, it will be in force until 31st December 2008, and can be extended in successive five-year periods as long as no reports are expressed by the signing parties with a minimum six month notice prior to the end of each period.

labour relations, understood not only as a source to regulate employment conditions but also as a method to order the running of the system itself.

In this respect, I ASEC draws up scenarios and anticipates guidelines of behaviour that the AINC will systematize and develop, in such a way that the former and the latter develop all their innovative power when they are analyzed as necessary and reciprocal complements of the renovation project started by the social actors. The contribution of I ASEC – and AINC, although this is an agreement that I shall only deal with sideways – to the process of building these initiatives can be illustrated by means of examining its roles.

The negotiation and signing of I ASEC was welcomed and positively judged by the Spanish scientific body as regards to the effects introduced in the composition of labour conflicts.[5] As it promoted and facilitated the establishment of means, different from the judicial path, I ASEC appeared to moderate the dominant model for solving conflicts: that is, the judicial model. By conferring the role of easing or reducing the high rate of 'judicialization' of the Spanish system of labour relations to this agreement, closing down the untidy role of the judge as an architect of this system, it offered a real approximation to its scope; albeit a partial and reductionist approximation.

As I already had the opportunity to state elsewhere,[6] the signing of the ASEC settled an old issue in our system: the predominance of the judicial method to satisfy collective controversies. However, the predominance of this model was only the logical corollary of the interaction of the structural elements that constitute the system of labour relations. In other words, the chronic difficulties and persistent failures of extrajudicial procedures in composing labour conflicts are a faithful reflection of a way of being and working of the system. As the Spanish Economic and Social Council rightfully stated,[7] the causes for the failure of these procedures have to be sought in deep-rooted problems of the system and not simply in deficiencies in its regulation.

In summary, the Spanish system of labour relations has focussed, at least until recently, on three basic elements: the configuration of state regulation as the preferential way of ordering the labour market; the analysis, treatment and solution of labour problems from essentially legal perspectives, and an individualistic conception and practice of labour relations in which the centre of gravity is focussed on the individual relationship between employee and employer. Each of these elements has produced a myriad of consequences that constitute the system. I shall mention some of the most significant ones.

The traditional and historical priority given to state mediation as the method to organize the system has been carried alongside, or has been accompanied by, an undeniable preference for a formula of judicial (or administrative) interpretation and implementation to the detriment of those formulae based on, or aimed

5 Amongst many others, see: Mercader Uguina (1996), 52 and Valdeolivas García (1997), 523.

6 See Valdes Dal-Ré (1998), 140.

7 Cf. CES (1994) 59.

at collective bargaining. Already in the constitutional period, the 'pseudo-legal value' assigned to collective bargaining has actively, though vaguely, collaborated to preserve this design. The legal paradigm of general-efficiency collective bargaining, in which the regulation aspect of the pact predominates opposed to the more exactly contractual dimension, reinforces the search of judicial settlements and weakens the autonomous ones.

On the other hand, the 'juridicism' with which these problems in the labour world are usually tackled and solved tends to devaluate the extra- or meta-juridical components. Nevertheless, those exert a greater influence on the decision-taking processes that constitute and mould labour relations. Stating the idea from the perspective of results, this 'juridicism' tends to stress the role of strictly juridical agents – judges and lawyers – as well as of the more 'juridified' means for the solution of conflicts and, therefore, devaluates the role of other type of agents and other instrumental forms.

Finally, the excessively individualistic consideration of labour relations has also helped to depreciate its collective aspect; that which puts the stress on the encounters that have taken place, the contacts that are established, the scenarios that are opened and the results obtained between collective subjects, instead of between the parties in a labour contract or, in other words, between an employer and a plurality of employees.

It is in this model – in its shortfalls and shortages – in which the excesses of judicialization have found its yeast and ferment. And, therefore, it is in this same context where the I ASEC also finds its real meaning, with the objective of not only substituting the judicial model of settling conflicts by means of changing the deciding subject, but also without altering the contents of the procedure by which the decision is made. If this had been its aim, the judgement regarding regulation of the means of composing collective conflicts would be reduced to a judgement of the efficiency, safety and satisfaction of the solution found.

The first and successive ASECs have sought something beyond and different to a mere changing of certain ways of composing conflict for others: administrative conciliation or *apud iudicem* and judicial sentence versus mere third-party proposals that are not invested with jurisdictional and private powers of their own accord, with binding strength and judgement. Encouragement of extrajudicial *formulae* is thus a simple pretext used by the ASECs to attain more ambitious purposes. For instance, converting collective autonomy into the centre of gravity of the model of labour relations as a whole, a model that does not reduce the role of collective agreement to a simple and sporadic occasion to regulate working conditions but that rises to become the method to develop and manage the rules for the system of labour relations.

Therefore, the strategic value of the ASECs consists in transcending the narrow limits that its *nomen* suggests and that its material content announces. The creation and development of extrajudicial means is not an end in itself. It is, quite the contrary, an instrument to reinforce collective bargaining, increasing the opportunities for a pact and 'the quality and efficiency of both the negotiating process and its result'.[8] This is, in short, the perspective from which the contribution of ASECs to the implementation of a model that truly places collective bargaining and all its consequences at the centre of rotation has to be judged. In addition, it is from this perspective and not the perspective, offered by mere de-judicialization that an assessment has to be made regarding whether this effort has had a positive result or, rather, whether the end result has been simple words isolated from any renovating content.

The purpose of this study focuses on the analysis of the most significant aspects, both organizational and procedural, that regulate extrajudicial means of solving collective conflict in Spain.[9] However, prior to carrying out the study stated, it seems appropriate to make some general considerations that contribute to a better understanding of the Spanish system for extrajudicial settlement of collective conflict.

As will be reasoned out below, procedures for the composition of labour controversies regulated by the successive ASECs do not constitute the only path to settle labour conflicts extra-judicially. Apart from these procedures, other systems that have their own different sources (either state or negotiation) also work. This plurality of paths is, however, not always articulated satisfactorily with concurrent conflicts that are not easily settled taking place occasionally.

In any case, I shall deal in this study with the procedures established in the ASECs exclusively. Stating the idea negatively, I will not deal with procedures established by regulations with a state origin[10] or with those others that, even when having a negotiation nature, have a territorial scope of regional implementation.[11]

2 Scope of implementation of ASEC

The scope of implementation of the successive ASECs has been limited by the co-ordinated and joint action of three criteria. The objective criterion that affects the controversial interest. The subjective criterion that relates to the quality of the parties in conflict and, finally, the territorial criterion. Each of these criteria poses a different problem that, consequently, needs to be tackled separately.

8 Cf. Del Rey Guanter (1995), 31.

9 See, amongst others, González-Posada (2001), Rodríguez Fernández (2003), 149 y Lantarón Barquín (2004).

10 The main principle is administrative conciliation that constitutes a compulsory stage in individual conflicts prior to access to social jurisdiction. For all and recently, see Garcia Quiñónês (2005).

11 In each of the 17 Spanish Autonomous Communities (regions), both sides of industry have negotiated multi-industry agreements that establish procedures for the extrajudicial settlement of labour conflicts that do not surpass the sphere of the Autonomous Community itself. For a comparative view of these agreements, see Sala Franco/Alfonso Mellado (2001).

2.1 The objective criterion

Article 1 of III ASEC currently constitutes the heading regulation that defines the material scope of implementation of the means to solve labour conflicts. Section 1 of this conventional passage states that the Agreement "[...] has the object of maintaining and developing a system to settle collective labour conflicts that arise between employers and employees or their corresponding bodies of representation".[12] The fact that individual conflicts are not included, implicitly deduced from a mere opposite interpretation of the content in the above statement, is repeated, although expressly this time, in Article 4.3 ASEC.

Even when the scope of implementation is limited to dealing with collective labour conflicts, not all controversies of this nature, however, are in effect subject to its jurisdiction. Article 4.1 of the Agreement states, by means of a list (to be understood as a closed list), which collective conflicts can be subjected to the settlement procedures designed in the contract regulation, as long as, the subjective and territorial elements concur. Specifically, the settlement procedures foreseen in III ASEC cover general types of collective conflict: juridical or interpretation conflicts on the one hand, and economic or interest conflicts on the other.[13] Nevertheless, these procedures do not cover all of these conflicts.

A) III ASEC is firstly applied to collective conflicts of interpretation and application which are susceptible to being settled by means of the special process of collective conflicts regulated in Article 151.1 LPL[14] (4.1.a). Without entering into a study of the notion of juridical collective conflict in procedural law, the limiting effects of the regulation remission carried out by successive ASECs can not go unnoticed as an expression of certain conventional laziness.

In the style required in the judicial process, this first category of collective conflicts requires the existence of a legitimate, current, specific, effective and controversial interest in order to activate the established means of settlement, where the intention is satisfied by the disappearance of the uncertainty situa-

---

12 Art. 4.1 I ASEC defined as its objective *"the creation* and development of a system (...)".

13 The 'juridical' collective conflict, those regarding rights, deals with the meaning and scope that has to be given to a formerly existing regulation (clause in collective bargaining or in an undertaking's agreement, for example), settling by means of the implementation of the objective interpretation criteria deduced from that regulation. The 'economic' conflict or conflict of 'interests' intends, directly or indirectly, to amend or substitute an existing regulation or, in some cases, to create a new and different one. See Vida Soria (1968), 38.

14 Art. 151.1 of the Law on Labour Procedure (LPL) establishes that "[...] lawsuits that affect the general interests of a generic group of employees and are based on the application of a state regulation, collective bargain, whatever its enforceability, or a decision or a business practice [...]" shall follow this process of collective conflict. For a greater understanding of this notion, see González-Posada (1993), 78 and Alfonso Mellado (1993), 64.

tion by means of an agreement signed through mediation or an arbitral award. With the regulation reference to Article 151 LPL in III ASEC (and previous ones), multi-industry agreements have systematically left conflicts of consultation outside their scope. This exclusion is justifiable from a judicial point of view but not from the extra-judicial dimension in which these agreements are now articulated. Thus, autonomous means of settlement are prevented from fulfilling, besides repairing roles, roles of prevention, avoidance or contention of the externalization of conflict situations. In any case, the negotiated option shows that ASECs have not managed to handle the main risk hovering over them with enough imagination: that of conceiving themselves as a 'mirror' of the collective conflict process, standing in line with it.

ASECs include conflicts over interpretation, not only of negotiation regulations[15] but also of state regulations in the sphere of implementation. However, for the latter, not all are included but only those of a strictly labour nature. Those controversies that arise in relation to the public social security system are not included.

B) Besides collective juridical conflicts, III ASEC covers collective conflicts over of interest. However, different to the technique used as regards to including interpretation controversies, which responds to the general clause model, the Agreement lists what type of economic conflicts and under what circumstances the provisions are applicable.

a) Firstly, 'conflicts that arise during the negotiation of collective bargaining or another collective agreement or pact' (Article 4.1.b III ASEC). These controversies have to be subjected to the means agreed as long as two requirements are met. The first of these, of a material nature, defines a certain quality in the nature of discrepancies existing between the parties, as these have to be significant, or using the terms arranged, they have to be 'substantial'. The second states a temporary rule, stating the condition that these extrajudicial procedures apply when these substantial differences have, moreover, caused a stopping of negotiations 'for a period of at least six months from' the constitution of the negotiation table. The fulfilment of this requirement, however, gives way if mediation is requested 'jointly' by those with the capacity to subscribe an agreement with *erga omnes* enforceability.[16]

---

[15] Any collective bargain or agreement, whatever its personal efficiency (general or limited), must be understood as negotiation regulation.

[16] The capacity to negotiate general enforceability agreements is defined by law, which distinguishes according to the sphere of agreement. In business agreements or those in lower spheres (work centres), this capacity is held, alternatively, by the elected bodies of representation (Works Council) or by trade union representatives (*shop steward*) that are present in these bodies. In sectoral agreements, the capacity is held only by trade unions and employers' associations, albeit not all of them, the most representative and representative in the sector exclusively.

The de facto situations that lead to the activation of the composition measures for this specific conflict manifestation, as finally described in the successive ASECs, have been defined in terms that express a conception that, paradoxically, is separated from that which informs the maintenance and development of the procedures established by multi-industry agreements themselves. The introduction of this temporary rule is equivalent to a solemn and formal declaration of the priority given by the parties involved to negotiation processes over the procedures regulated in ASEC. However, this is a point of view contaminated by the 'juridicism' that perverts our system of labour relations and on top of that it expresses a bad faith in the strength of the procedures that are established to constitute a system that is based on dialogue.

The ultimate design sought by the ASEC, as reasoned above, is to introduce the contractual principle as a backbone to the running of our system of labour relations. From this perspective, the processes of collective bargaining and procedures to settle the conflicts that arise in the development of these systems can not be understood as realities that are rigidly separated by neither material reasons or, even less, temporary reasons. Autonomous procedures for the composition of controversies offer new possibilities for the parties to continue their contractual encounters and, therefore, offer renewed opportunities to reach agreements. In short, when conflict arises in a negotiation process, transition from negotiation to the procedure to settle the conflict should have been configured in a flowing, flexible manner, contrary to formalism, that is, in terms that are exactly opposite to how they have been carried out.

The establishment of a six-month waiting period between the verification of a substantial difference and a situation where the negotiation process is blocked as a result of this verification tends to distort, in practice, the autonomous nature of this conflict that may probably end up taking refuge and dissolving in the conflict generated from taking industrial action. In order to fight the situation of negotiation obstruction and to expedite the rate of negotiation, workers' representatives will, occasionally have no other way out than to resort to instruments of collective self-protection. In this sense, and paradoxically, the ASEC promotes and encourages or may promote and encourage controversial formulae to manage the processes of collective negotiation.

In any case, and beside what will be stated below, the rule in Article 4.1.b III ASEC can be reinterpreted in view of the provisions contained in national sectoral agreements. These agreements, following indications established in multi-industry agreements on collective bargaining since 1997, may have included a code of conduct in negotiation that encompasses, amongst other aspects, 'procedures and paths to avoid blocking and breaking-offs in negotiation processes, agreeing maximum periods of process paralyzing, at the end of which the parties' have to submit to processes established in the ASEC.[17] In this

[17] These were the terms used by the ANIC 1997. See Casas Baamonde (1998). And are also the terms that appear in later Agreements on Collective Bargaining 2002, 2003 and 2004. See Rodríguez-Piñero/Valdes Dal-Ré/Casas Baamonde (2002) and Valdes Dal-Ré (2003a).

sense, national-scale collective agreements may, therefore, re-devise the rules to specify what is understood as blocked negotiation towards a direction of greater operating capacity, from a practical point of view, and more coherent with the objectives and interests served by the ASECs from the perspective of systemic construction.

b) Conflicts that lead to industrial action or that arise from the determination of security and maintenance services in the case of industrial action are also under the jurisdiction of ASEC (arts. 4.1.c. III ASEC).

A strictly grammatical interpretation of the conventional passages transcribed could lead to an understanding that we are facing two types of perfectly different disputes. The use of the disjunctive particle 'or' would confirm this. Such a hypothesis is immediately discarded through an understanding in the prior regulation statement adapted to procedural rules that organize the right of industrial action or, similarly, the stages that industrial action follows from a logical-systemic perspective. III ASEC, in the style of its predecessors, is indeed formulating two modes of conflicts: industrial action and establishment of safety and maintenance services in the case of industrial action. However, the latter does not appear as an alternative to the first. It constitutes a bonus or an addition that may possibly accompany it.

To the effects of being included in the scope of implementation of ASEC, the deciding factor is not the nature of the controversy but the mere call to industrial action: that is, the announcement or call for collective and arranged abstention from work, independent of the objective sought by industrial action or of the manner of its execution. Consequently, the content of the dispute that is outwardly expressed through industrial action can lie indistinctly amongst juridical conflicts or economic conflicts. In those cases where the conflict lies in fixing maintenance and security services associated to a call to industrial action, the condition of this conflict over interests is not debatable – in principle.

c) 'Conflicts derived from disagreements arising in the consultation period' that is legally established (arts. 4.1.d. III ASEC).

The clear terms of these precepts do not give rise to doubts on the limits of the latter mode of conflicts affected by the scope of implementation of ASECs, which encloses a plurality of controversies. All of them have a common element in that the dispute is born at the heart of a procedure whose aim is to confer worker representatives in the undertaking the opportunity to reach an agreement with the employer regarding the measures to be adopted in issues of reorganization in the volume of employment in the undertaking (redundancy) or of a substantial amendment to certain employment conditions.

2.2 The subjective criterion

Not all collective conflicts, as they have been limited by objective reasons, have to be settled according to procedures established by III ASEC. Article 1.2 of the Agreement excludes from its jurisdiction those collective conflicts in which one of the parties is a public administration (state, autonomous community, local entity or autonomous body dependent on one of these), even when the material element concurs.

This exclusion, based on one of the parties in the conflict being a public administrative body, is caused by motives of opportunity and convenience. But in any case, we must point out that Spanish legislation does not prevent collective conflicts arising between a public administrative body and its staff from being settled by means of extrajudicial procedures.

2.3 The territorial criterion

The last of the limiting criteria in the scope of implementation of III ASEC is of a territorial nature. Specifically, procedures established in the current ASEC can be exclusively implemented in relation to two types of collective conflicts: a) those that are sectoral, or within an activity, that surpasses the sphere of an Autonomous Community; and b) those in the undertaking, as long as it affects several work centres based in different Autonomous Communities and that are, if it is a conflict of interpretation of a conventional regulation, within the undertaking or inferior 'but superior to each of the work centres affected' (Article 4.2). Other controversies, different to those stated, are not covered by the ASEC.

Even though the general scope of these co-ordination regulations have their natural sphere of implementation between the ASEC and regional agreements in the same field, they, nevertheless do not manage to solve all practical problems that arise. This is due to the fact that these agreements also define their own scope of implementation based on criteria of a territorial nature, criteria that respond to three different rules, instead of being uniform. These rules are the following: a) that in the sphere in which it has effect, the solution to the conflict does not exceed the autonomous community; b) that the undertakings' headquarters are based in the autonomous community and affects the employees offering their services there and c) that the undertaking, besides being based in the community territory, is affected by an agreement with a regional or inferior scope.[18]

In regional agreements that follow the double jurisdiction of the undertaking and of services offered, the supra-regional sectoral or undertaking controversy can be settled, projected unto the autonomous community, by procedures of a lesser territorial sphere, thus opening a situation of true conventional concurrence.

The First Additional Provision of III ASEC states to this effect a rule to compose concurrent conflicts, addressed to the will of the parties affected by which they will choose by consensus the applicable agreement: the concur-

[18] Respectively, the agreements of Galicia, Madrid and Balearic Islands (a), Canary Islands, Catalonia and Basque Country (b) a Community of Valencia (c). See Sala Franco/Alfonso Mellado (1996) 183.

rent state or regional agreement. This is a precarious rule, the implementation of which opens up a flood of juridical problems, amongst others the relevant problem of distinguishing the exact placing of legal provisions on the solution of concurrent conflicts between collective bargaining and agreements.

3 The procedures to settle labour conflicts

3.1 Organization

Since its first appearance, ASECs have deposited the organization and administrative management of procedures to compose collective labour conflicts to a peer institution: the Inter-confederate Service of Mediation and Arbitration (*SIMA*). The *SIMA* has juridical personality and capacity to take action and its formal juridical form is that of a foundation under the auspices of the Ministry of Employment and Social Affairs. Its economic resources come from public funding as it is financed through the state budget, and its activity is free of charge for employees and employers.

The *SIMA*, like any other foundation, is directed by a Board of Trustees, made up of representatives of the parties signing the ASECs 'in equal numbers'. The Board of Trustees is headed by a President, who can be one of the members of the aforementioned parties or may be 'designated by mutual agreement' of the parties. Until now, the presidency has been exercised, by means of a rotation system, by the representatives signing the successive agreements.

In accordance with Article 6.5 of III ASEC, the *SIMA* 'will only harbour mediation and arbitration suits derived from what is agreed in the present Agreement'. With this wording, this conventional clause formulates the principle that may be designated as contractual legality. In the exercise of its roles, the *SIMA* is strictly subject to the contents established in the ASEC. The Service cannot accept submission of conflicts that due to objective, subjective or territorial reasons fall outside the scope of implementation of the Agreement. Neither can the Service introduce procedures to compose conflicts different to those agreed nor can it organize procedures agreed according to criteria different to those collectively agreed. The principle of contractual legality has a principle of uniformity in the means to reach settlements associated to it, extended to all of its aspects or facets. III ASEC does not regulate other procedures other than mediation or arbitration. Both must be arranged according to the provisions agreed.

Furthermore, drawing up a list of mediators and arbitrators proposed by the parties signing the ASEC also corresponds to the *SIMA*. On the other hand, it corresponds to the parties in conflict to designate a mediator, with one acting for each side or, in the case of 'mutual agreement', agree the appointment of only one. Similarly, they have to designate an arbitrator or establish an association made up of an odd number of arbitrators. Given the case that the parties do not proceed to appoint the mediators or arbitrators, this competence will be taken on by the *SIMA* (Article 7.2 III ASEC).

3.2 Intervention of the Joint Commission of collective bargaining

The III ASEC, reproducing the criteria in previous agreements, establishes that, in conflicts of interpretation of a collective bargain, the intervention of the Joint Commission (JC) will be required. This provision also extends to controversies of implementation of 'other collective agreements or pacts', in any event that the JC is the established body of administration and management (Article 10.1). Submission of the conflict to the JC thus establishes a mandatory requirement prior to the promotion of the procedures agreed.

To my mind, the basic roles played by this procedure foreseen by III ASEC unto the JC are two. Firstly, and probably the most relevant, consists in securing the composition of conflict at the heart of the peer body which is entrusted, in general, with the interpretation of collective bargaining due to a constant and consolidated contractual experience. The intervention of the JC constitutes a guarantee in the unity of interpretation of the contractual instrument over which discrepancies exist. The intention of this intervention, secondly, is to exhaust a procedure that, given the case, acts as a requirement to promote actions before labour judges and courts.[19]

3.3 General principles

With the clarifications made regarding the intervention of the JC, procedures for the settlement of collective conflicts established since the first ASEC have been two. Specifically, ASECs have not followed the classic triad in the means to compose labour conflicts, made up of conciliation/mediation/arbitration, committing to a simpler outline, made up of mediation and interpretation exclusively.

In the design of ASEC, mediation and arbitration are not configured as procedures to be used interchangeably. Indeed, mediation is defined as an ordinary medium to access the system of extrajudicial composition for collective controversies. Mediation, however, does not provide for a compulsory path towards arbitration when it ends without reaching an agreement, as this step is in any case voluntary (Article 8 III ASEC), neither does subjecting the dispute to arbitration formulae imply a prior exhausting of the mediation stage (Article 18.2 del III ASEC). ASECs have established a closed and self-sufficient system to settle conflict. The means, however, that constitute and structure the system are not aligned. Their reciprocal relationships respond to a model that is technically less hampered or, in other words, more plural. A model that allows the parties

---

[19] For further detail, Rodríguez Fernández (2001) 209 and Valdes Dal-Ré (2003) 21.

the possibility to choose amongst a variety of itineraries instead of following just one route. Besides the intervention of the Peer Commission, the parties in conflict may make successive and scaling use of mediation and arbitration. They may also resort to mediation, without progressing in the path of ASEC or, similarly, abandoning its path to enter the judicial path or, in short, getting around mediation and ending, except in the path of contestation, the judicial settlement.

Considering this from another perspective, all procedures established in the ASEC are subject to some principles stated in Article 9 and which many other conventional clauses in the Agreement repeat or develop. 'Free of charge, speed, procedure equality, parties' audience, contradiction and impartiality' makes up a myriad of the so-called 'governing principles' in the means of extrajudicial settlement. This is a formulation that does not come without serious, objective criticisms, appreciated from diverse points of view. Ultimately, the establishment of these principles reveals a paradoxical mimicry between extrajudicial and judicial procedures.

Leaving free-of-charge and speed aside, the validity of the remaining principles only has sense in a type of procedure in which a third party other than the parties in conflict is summoned. This third party, as director of the procedure, is required to be impartial and not to make decisions inaudita parte or to grant both parties the same opportunities to defend their interests. Nevertheless, not all procedures contemplated by the ASEC have the presence of a third party, other than the parties in conflict, associated to them. Indeed, the CP of the collective bargain does not have or does not always have this condition. The nature of the intervention of this peer body is not singular, behaving sometimes as a mediating third party and, at other times, as simple locus of a direct and bilateral negotiation between the parties in conflict.

Moving the focus of our reasoning from the perspective of juridical construction to a more practical sphere, the universal value that ASEC intends to confer to the aforementioned principles does not prevent a raise to objections. The implementation of these principles to '(all) procedures foreseen in this Agreement' is an expression of the option of a policy of law carried out by the parties signing the ASEC and consists in proceeding with an undifferentiated treatment of mediation and arbitration. However, this option and how it is regulated is or may become dysfunctional for mediation, which requires a flexible, almost informal field game in order to reach stable and long-lasting performance. As it corresponds, in the end, to a means of composing conflicts where the parties affected play the prominent role.

3.4 Mediation

The mediation process responds to an almost informal logic. It starts in writing presented by the subjects that have acknowledged legitimacy to promote the procedure.[20] From this initiation script, which must contain some minimum indications[21] and in which the mediator may be designated, it is transferred to the other party that may, likewise, proceed to the appointment of the mediator. The mediation act is compulsory and, once established, and during the length of the procedure, the call for industrial action or the adoption of lock-out measures is prohibited together with the exercise of judicial or administrative actions and, more generally, any other action aimed at settling the conflict.

The appointed mediator or mediators have to summon the parties for, at least, one appearance, guaranteeing the principles of audience, equality and contradiction. Mediators are obliged to draw up proposals to settle the conflict, including submission to arbitration. The parties are free to reject or accept the proposal. In case of acceptance, the mediation agreement has the same efficiency than the contents agreed in collective bargain. In addition, in the case of non-observance, compliance can be required by procedures of execution of judicial sentences.

3.5 Arbitration

The arbitration procedure contemplated in III ASEC is of a voluntary nature. The voluntary nature of arbitration procedures is linked to a principle of separation between the source establishing arbitration, the ASEC, and the arbitration commitment that is born each time that a collective conflict arises and that the parties have to endorse at that time precisely. This division explains that the arbitration procedure – and I speak of the procedure and not the arbitration decision – binds those that have signed the precedent commitment.

The regulation that both legislation and the ASECs carry out on the efficiency of the decision constitutes another of the controversial issues, probably the most controversial. Without going into depth on the subject raised,[22] the answer to the question raised is not unitary or, likewise, depends on the type of collective conflict submitted to an arbitration procedure.

20 These subjects vary depending on the nature of conflict. In this sense and in relation to conflicts of interpretation or juridical conflicts, they are legitimate if the conflict is of the undertaking, elected bodies of representation, the trade union as well as the employer; and if the conflict is of a higher level, trade unions and employers' associations "[...] whose scope of activity corresponds to or is higher than the conflict [...]". In collective conflicts of interest, Art. 13 III ASEC has special rules.

21 Identification of the parties in conflict, the object of conflict, employees affected and territorial sphere.

22 For further detail, see Valdes Dal-Ré (2001) 189.

For a start, and in relation with collective conflicts of interpretation, paragraph 3 of Article 91 ET (Workers' Statute) states that the decision will have the juridical efficiency of the collective bargains regulated by the ET, as long as the arbitration compromise has been signed by those with the legitimacy to agree to the manner of collective bargain. Moreover, Article 85 ET states that the decisions ruled in procedures that have arisen from discrepancies occurring in the consultation period will have the same efficiency than the agreements reached in this procedure, thus establishing a correspondence between agreement and decision.[23] The sector within the doctrine that believes that reorganization agreements, as opposed to regulating agreements, lack the efficiency of bargains is probably right. In any case, it is reasonable to understand that, in these hypotheses, the arbitration decision will have to be adopted in accordance with the regulations that rule the adoption of agreements during the consultation period: by the majority of members of the unitary representation or, given the case, by trade union sections that represent the majority of this representation. Lastly, the ET does not provide for the efficiency of decisions that solve the remaining conflicts that can be settled, in accordance with the ASEC, by means of arbitration. In the cases of arbitration derived from conflicts arising in the blocking of negotiation, the decision settles the conflict of interest and, for this reason, must have the efficiency belonging to a collective bargain. As we are dealing with arbitrations motivated by the call for industrial action, the decision must have the efficiency of the agreement that ends this call: that is, it will only affect the organization that has adopted the decision and, consequently, the possible judgement to call off industrial action only binds those who undersigned the corresponding arbitration commitment. However, a different settlement arises from the conflict generated by the establishment of security and maintenance services. The arbitration decision, by being undersigned by the majority of worker representatives, has general efficiency.

Otherwise, Additional Provision 7 of the LPL establishes the comparison, to the effect of execution, between firm sentences and equally firm decisions, if these are pronounced by the body that can be constituted by means of multi-industry agreements or collective bargains of Article 83 ET. In view of this comparison, regulations regarding provisional execution whilst a possible contestation is settled can not be applied on arbitration decisions. Furthermore, judicial execution of the decision is deferred as long as the deadline for contestation has not been met, set by the III ASEC at thirty days in general (Article 22.3). The causes for contestation of decisions are valued to be the following suppositions: when the arbitrator or arbitrators have settled on an issue that is not subject to arbitration decision, when the principles that regulate the arbitration

[23] However, the Spanish legislator will introduce a statement expressing a rational unfeasibility when making the decision since it settles a problem and opens a new one as the Law itself does not define the efficiency of agreements reached in the consultation period.

procedure have not been complied with (for example, the principle of audience of parties), when the decision is pronounced after the established deadline and, finally, when the decision itself contains settlements that contradict constitutional or legal regulations.

Bibliography

ALFONSO MELLADO (1993)
Alfonso Mellado, C.L., *Proceso de conflicto colectivo*, Valencia (Tirant lo Blanch)

CASAS BAAMONDE, M.E. (1998)
Casas Baamonde, M.E., "El Acuerdo Interconfederal sobre Negociación Colectiva: continuidad e innovación de contenidos y propuestas de reforma de la estructura de la negociación colectiva", in Rodríguez-Pinero,M./Valdés Dal-Ré, F./Casas Baamonde, M.E. (Coords.), *Estabilidad en el empleo, diálogo social y negociación colectiva*, Madrid (Ed. Tecnos), pp. 190-226

CONSEJO ECONÓMICO Y SOCIAL (1994)
Consejo Económico Y Social, *Informe sobre procedimientos autónomos de conflictos Laborales*, Madrid (Ed. CES)

DEL REY GUANTER, S. (1995)
Del Rey Guanter, S., "Medios extrajudiciales de solución de conflictos", in AA.VV., *Solución extrajudicial de conflictos laborales*, Madrid (Pub. del CES de la Comunidad de Madrid), pp. 20-43

DEL REY GUANTER, S. (1996)
Del Rey Guanter, S., "El Acuerdo sobre Solución Extrajudicial de Conflictos Laborales: un análisis inicial", in AA.VV., *La aplicación de la reforma del Estatuto de los Trabajadores en la negociación colectiva*, Madrid (Ed. MTAS), pp. 99-128

GARCÍA QUIÑÓNES, J.C. (2005)
García Quiñónes, J.C., *La conciliación laboral*, Valladolid (Ed. Lex-Nova)

GONZÁLEZ-POSADA, E. (1993)
González-Posada, E., *El proceso de conflicto colectivo de trabajo*, Madrid (Acarl)

GONZÁLEZ-POSADA, E. (Director) (2001)
González-Posada, E., *La solución extrajudicial de los conflictos laborales, Valladolid* (Junta de Castilla y León)

LANTARÓN BARQUÍN, D. (2004)
Lantarón Barquín, D., *La solución extrajudicial de los conflictos de trabajo*, Valladolid (Ed. Lex-Nova)

MERCADER UGUINA, J. (1996)
Mercader Uguina, J., "El Acuerdo sobre Solución Extrajudicial de Conflictos Laborales: un paso importante en la solución de un problema pendiente", *Relaciones Laborales* núm. 9, pp. 50-72

RODRÍGUEZ FERNÁNDEZ, M.L. (2001)
Rodríguez Fernández, M.L., "La intervención previa de la Comisión Paritaria en los procedimientos del ASEC-II", en González-Posada, E. (Director) *La solución extrajudicial de los conflictos laborales*, Valladolid (Junta de Castilla y León), pp. 209-257

RODRÍGUEZ FERNÁNDEZ, M.L. (2003)
Rodríguez Fernández, M.L., "Conciliación, mediación y arbitraje en España", in Valdés Dal-Ré, F. (dir.), *Conciliación, mediación y arbitraje en los países de la Unión Europea*, Madrid (Ed. MTAS) pp. 149-214

RODRÍGUEZ-PIÑERO, M./VALDES DAL-RÉ, F./CASAS BAMONDE, M.E. (20002)
Rodríguez-Piñero, M./Valdes Dal-Ré, F./Casas Bamonde, M.E., "El Acuerdo Interconfederal para la Negociación Colectiva", *Relaciones Laborales* núm. 2, pp. 1-18

SALA FRANCO, T./ALFONSO MELLADO, C.L. (1996)
Sala Franco, T./Alfonso Mellado, C.L., *Los procedimientos extrajudiciales de solución de los conflictos laborales establecidos en la negociación colectiva*, Valencia (Ed. Tirant lo Blanch)

SALA FRANCO, T./ALFONSO MELLADO, C.L. (2001)
Sala Franco, T./Alfonso Mellado, C.L., *Los acuerdos estatal y autonómicos sobre solución extrajudicial de conflictos laborales*, Madrid (Ed. CES)

VALDEOLIVAS GARCÍA, Y. (1997)
Valdeolivas García, Y., "El Acuerdo sobre Solución Extrajudicial de Conflictos Laborales: la superación de una asignatura pendiente", in Valdés Dal-Ré, F. (Dir.), *La reforma pactada de las legislaciones laboral y de Seguridad Social*, Valladolid (Ed. Lex-Nova), pp. 523-567

VALDES DAL-RÉ, F. (1998)
Valdes Dal-Ré, F., "Cuestiones y problemas aplicativos del Acuerdo sobre Solución Extrajudicial de Conflictos Laborales (ASEC)", in AA.VV., *La nueva función de la negociación colectiva y los Acuerdos Interconfederales de empleo*, Madrid (Ed. MTAS), pp. 137-163

VALDES DAL-RÉ, F. (2001)
Valdes Dal-Ré, F., "Arbitraje y conflictos colectivos en el ASEC: problemas de aplicación", en González-Posada, E. (Director) *La solución extrajudicial de los conflictos laborales*, Valladolid (Junta de Castilla y León), pp. 189-207

VALDES DAL-RÉ, F. (2003a
Valdes Dal-Ré, F., "El Acuerdo Interconfederal para la Negociación Colectiva 2003", *Relaciones Laborales* núm. 9, pp. 1-15

VALDES DAL-RÉ, F. (2003b)
Valdes Dal-Ré, F., "La solución de los conflictos colectivos de interpretación y aplicación por las Comisiones Paritarias de los convenios colectivos", in AA.VV., *Mediación y arbitraje en España. El papel de las Comisiones Paritarias*, Madrid (Ed. UGT), pp. 17-44

VIDA SORIA, J. (1968)
Vida Soria, J., "La distinción entre conflictos sobre derechos y conflictos sobre intereses en la problemática general de los conflictos colectivos de trabajo", in AA.VV., *Quince lecciones sobre conflictos colectivos de trabajo*, Madrid (Pub. Facultad de Derecho), pp. 33-50

Questionnaire

I To what extent (if at all) are employment relations in the public sector in your country distinguished from employment relations in the private sector?

II In your country, which facilities are provided (by the state and/or both sides of industry) for assisting parties in resolving collective labour disputes (e.g. by offering mediation services)? How do these facilities operate in practice? Do these facilities satisfy a distinct need?

III Do facilities differ for the public and private sector respectively?

IV In your country, do any restrictions apply to the public sector employees' right to strike? If so, are such restrictions in any way compensated by alternative procedures or options for these employees?

V In case the said facilities have been institutionalized (recently), would you say that institutionalization has contributed to a gain in time / a more swift handling of (imminent) disputes?

VI Has institutionalization amounted to a restriction of the right to strike?

VII Has institutionalization of mediation as a remedial intervention technique, contributed to the prevention of disputes (e.g. where disputes mediated were identified as symptomatic for underlying, structural problems in a particular company, and advisory work was undertaken by way of follow-up?)

VIII How important do you regard branch-specific knowledge in a mediator?

IX Against the backdrop of emerging EU collective agreements and genuine European companies, what would be the best way to deal with cross-border collective labour disputes in the nearby future?

X How should the requirements imposed by Article 6, section 3 of the 1961 European Social Charter be met?
(Art. 6 s. 3 reads: With a view to ensuring the effective exercise of the right to bargain collectively, the Contracting Parties undertake: [...] to promote the establishment and use of appropriate machinery for conciliation and voluntary arbitration for the settlement of labour disputes).

XI How are the facilities in your country being financed? How many staff (full-time, part-time, other) are involved?

XII Is there a professional body of knowledge, or are there particular insights, in the areas of dispute resolution and/or collective bargaining, that could have relevance for the new EU Member States?

Contributors

Contributors

Alex Brenninkmeijer
National Ombudsman of the Netherlands and formerly a professor appointed to the Albeda-chair at the University of Leyden.

Kurt Eriksson
Legal Counsel, Medlingsinstitutet, Stockholm

Frank Hendrickx
Professor of labour law, Faculty of Law, University of Leuven

Rob Jagtenberg
Associate professor of comparative law, Faculty of Law, Erasmus University Rotterdam

Terry Lippiatt
Director of Mediation Services, Advisory Conciliation and Arbitration Service, London

Jan Rombouts
Director General, Federal Ministry of Employment, Labour and Social Dialogue, Brussels, and Visiting Professor, Social Research Unit, Faculty of Law, University of Antwerp

Annie de Roo
Associate professor of comparative law, Faculty of Law, Erasmus University Rotterdam and mediator

Loe Sprengers
Professor at the University of Leyden, appointed to the Albeda-chair

Juhani Salonius
National Conciliator, Helsinki

Fernando Valdés Dal-Ré
Professor of labour law, Universidad Complutense de Madrid

Ulrich Zachert
Professor of labour law, University of Hamburg

Other participants at the expert meeting

Irene Asscher-Vonk
Professor of labour Law, Faculty of Law, University of Nijmegen

Joan Bloemaerts
Senior Advisor, Federation of Trade Unions FNV, Amsterdam

René Blijlevens
Senior Advisor Social Affairts, Confederation of Netherlands Industry and Employers VNO-NCW, The Hague

Caroline Koetsenruijter
Member of staff, Alternative Dispute Resolution project, University of Leyden

Claudia Staal
Directorate International Affairs, Ministry of Social Affairs and Employment, The Hague

Evert Verhulp
Professor of Labour Law, University of Amsterdam

Due to unforeseen commitments, Mr Bloemaerts and Mrs Staal could not attend the meeting in person. They did however express their continuing interest in the subject.

14W78473/ T1/ 9789076871615